The Black & White Book

Shawn M. Tomlinson's Guide to Photography
Volume 4

by

shawn m tomlinson

2015

The Black & White Book

B&W Photography in the 21st Century

Shawn M. Tomlinson's
Guide to Photography
Volume 4

© 2014, 2015 by Shawn M. Tomlinson
Zirlinson Publishing

ISBN: 978-1-329-20465-2

Dedication

This volume is dedicated to all those who taught me about photography directly and indirectly over the years, including Harold Laird, Spencer Tulis, Bill Trojan, Gary W. Ziroli, Richard H. Nilsen, William D. Bonafede, J.D. Canell, Ansel Adams, Imogen Cunningham, Kai Man Wong, Lok Cheung, Alamby Leung, Tony & Chelea Northrup, Ken Rockwell, the writers at DP Review and many, many others.

For what it's worth,
thank you all.

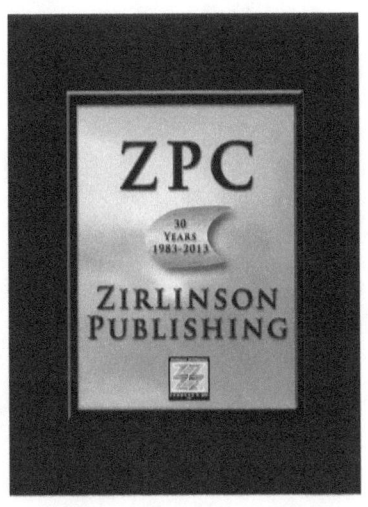

The Black & White Book

Shawn M. Tomlinson's Guide to Photography Volume 4

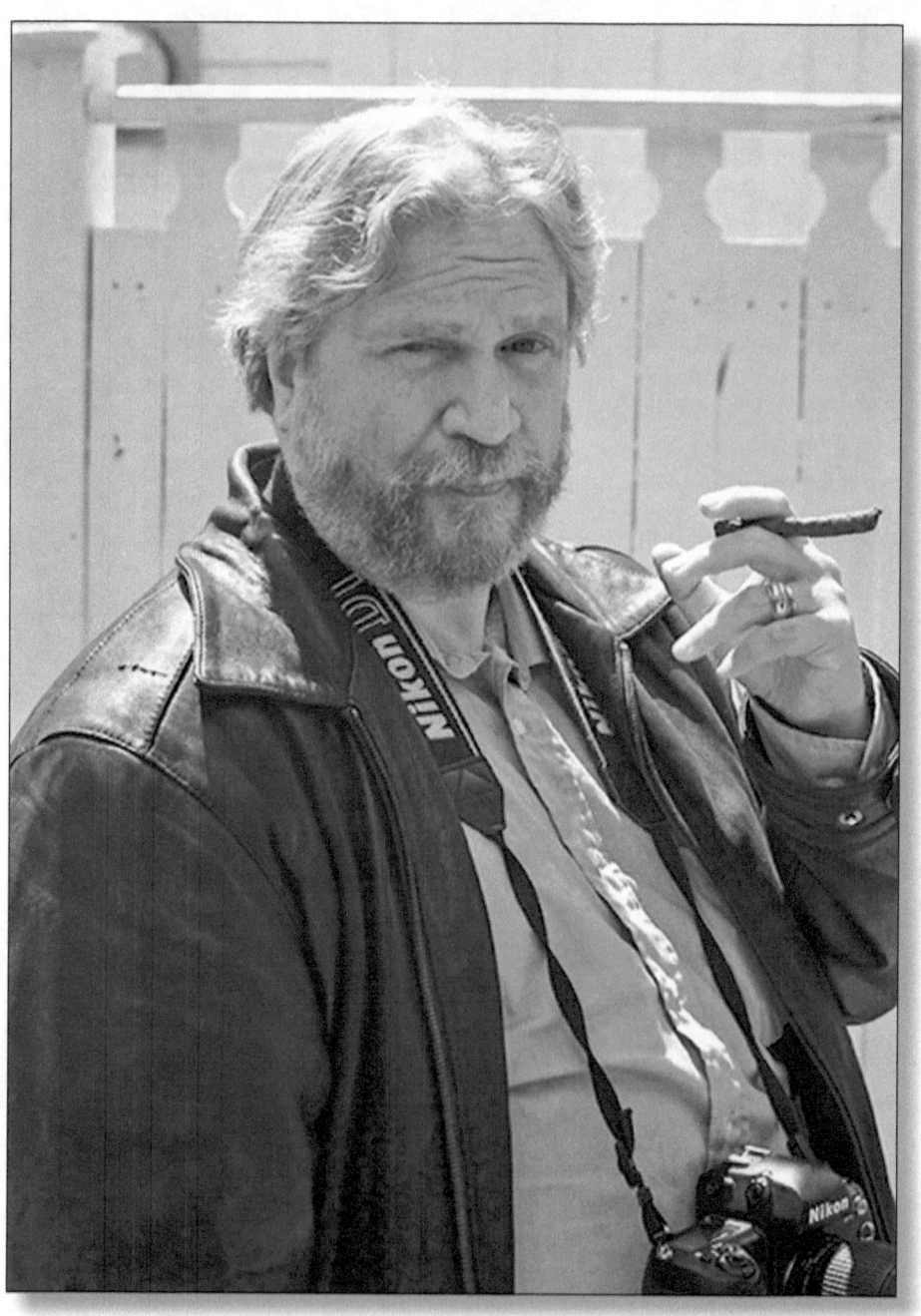

Shawn M. Tomlinson, Saratoga Springs, NY, May 17, 2014.
Nikon D1X, 46mm, 1/500, f/4.5, ISO 200, Av, Pattern Metering
Photo © 2014 by Gary W. Ziroli

Contents

Read *The Black & White Book* on the go with this special offer!

The Black & White Book also is available as an eBook for Kindle and other devices. If you purchase this paperback or hard cover copy, you are eligible for a special deal on the eBook version. The Kindle version (ASIN: B00QW5P9UI) is priced at $2.99, but if you own this actual book, you can get the eBook version for 99¢. Just visit Amazon.com (http://www.amazon.com/gp/product/B00QW5P9UI?*Version*=1&*entries*=0) for details. The eBook version includes the duotone versions of some of the images printed here as well.

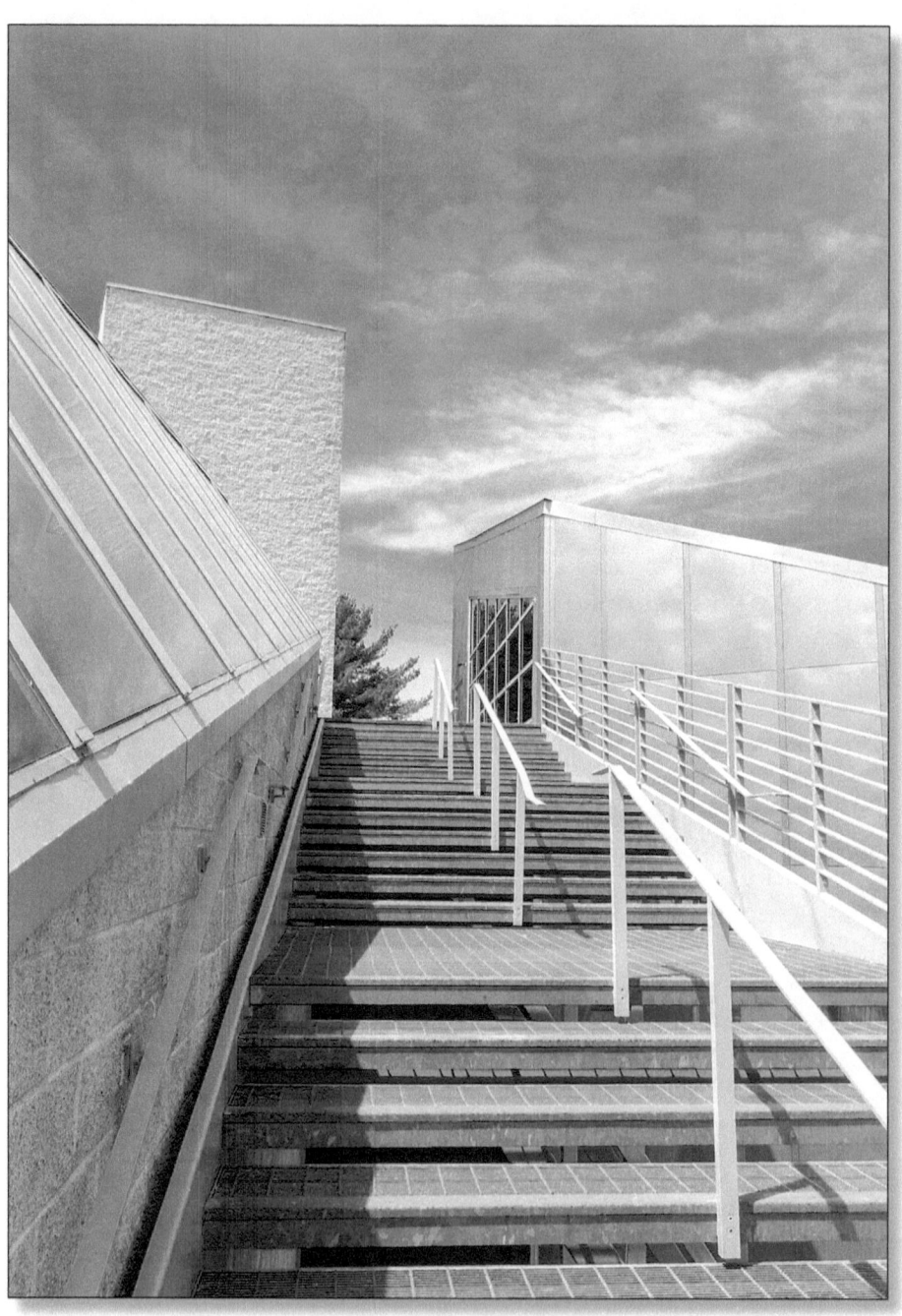

Tang Museum, Skidmore, Saratoga Springs, NY, May 9, 2015.
Nikon D7000, 10mm, 1/640, f/10, ISO 250, Tv, pattern metering
Photo © 2015 by Shawn M. Tomlinson

The Black & White Book

Shawn M. Tomlinson's Guide to Photography
Volume 4

by

shawn m tomlinson

2015

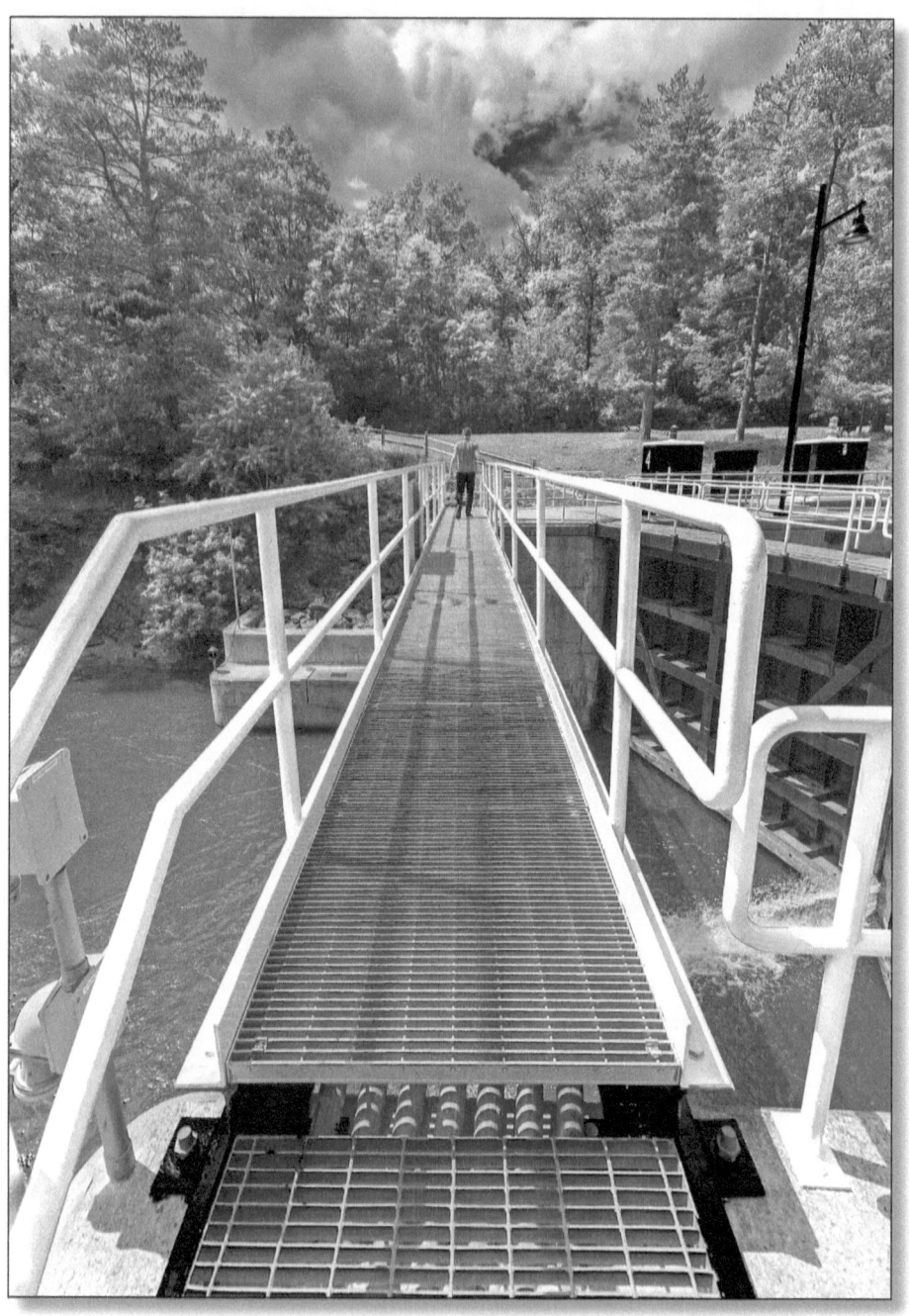

Lock C-4, Stillwater, NY, June 13, 2015.
Nikon D2x, 10mm, 1/1000, f/6.7, ISO 400, Tv, Pattern Metering
Photo © 2015 by Shawn M. Tomlinson

Introduction

I was a little surprised to find that the original eBook of The Black & White Books was relatively popular when it appeared. Particularly in Great Britain, for some reason.

I guess it just proves that I am not the only idiosyncratic curmudgeon in the 21st century.

These guide books for photography started because I got asked the same questions often, and I thought that, as a writer and editor, as well as a photographer, for most of my life, I would put the information into a format people could read.

Without asking me.

Although, I do enjoy talking about photographic technique endlessly...

Still, this is a reasonably short guide for beginners about how and when to shoot images that can be great in black and white. I try to cover all the necessary information without making anything too technical, although certain things simply are technical.

A friend and photographic colleague of mine, Richard Nilsen, often complains that I am too concerned with the technical aspects of photography.

Perhaps, but it is important to know how things work to make them work the way you want them to. When I see a photograph I really like, I immediately start trying to figure out how the photographer did it. I don't always use what I discover, but if I know how to do it, I can do it.

That's the point here.

Just taking a color photo and hitting Grayscale Mode will, in fact, produce an OK grayscale image. I'm sure that if the stars align correctly and the designated sacrifices to the photography gods are made, once in a great while, this will produce a great image.

The odds go up fast, though, if you do not just use the

Grayscale Mode.

Thinking in black and white while shooting photos, as well as knowing how to get the absolute best image in processing will turn an OK grayscale image into a stunner.

Not all images are stunners, of course. And not all photos work well in black and white.

The ones that do, however, can really say something to the viewer, make the viewer *feel*.

To me, that is worth getting a little technical and working to make my black and white images the best they can be.

Part of that is seeing that a photo does not work in black and white and being content with the color version.

For the photos that do really work in black and white or duotone, well, there's just nothing else like them.

Shawn M. Tomlinson
May 30, 2015
Ballston Lake, NY

Some Notes

The cutlines (captions) for each photo may be a bit confusing if you are not accustom to the way camera data is written. So, let me clarify using this as a sample:

Ballston Lake, NY, May 18, 2015.
Nikon D2x, 300mm, 1/800, f/5.6, ISO 400, Tv, pattern metering
Photo © 2015 by Shawn M. Tomlinson

The first line is obvious. The photo was taken at Ballston Lake, NY, on May 18, 2015. The second line means that the image was shot with the Nikon D2x digital single-lens reflex camera at 300mm with a 1/800th of a second shutter speed. The aperture was set at f/5.6 and the ISO sensitivity to 400. Tv signifies shutter priority mode on some cameras. It is S on others. Tv is more distinctive, so I use it for every camera. You also may see P, M or Av listed. P is program mode, Av is aperture-priority mode, not "Auto." I never shoot in "Auto." Pattern metering means the meter was set to pattern rather than spot or center-weighted.

The
Black &
White
Book

Shawn M. Tomlinson's
Guide to Photography
Volume 4

by

shawn m tomlinson

2015

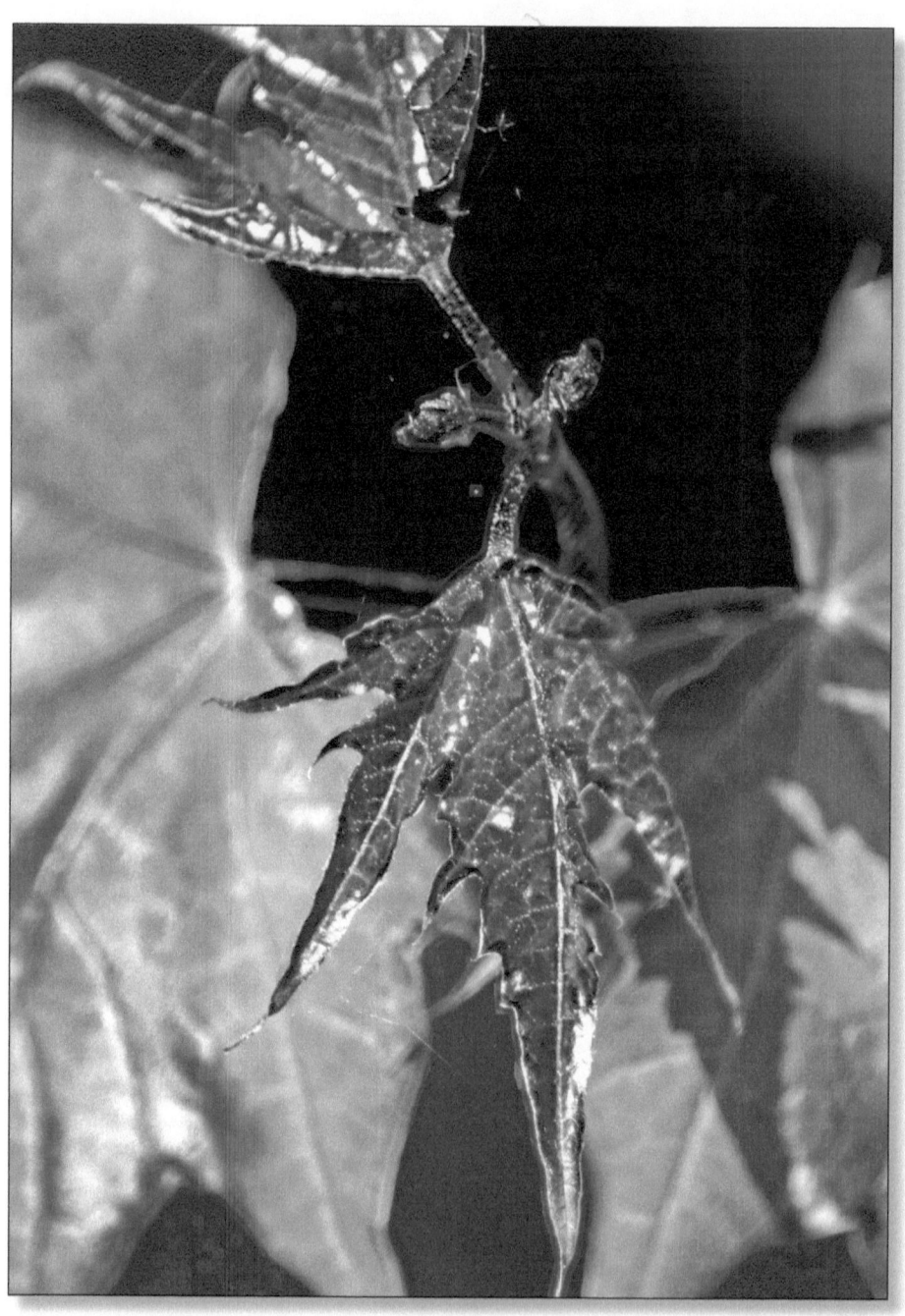

Ballston Lake, NY, May 18, 2015.
Nikon D2x, 300mm, 1/800, f/5.6, ISO 400, Tv, pattern metering
Photo © 2015 by Shawn M. Tomlinson

First Words

A crazy, self-involved woman I knew in Berkeley, once said to me that the very act of writing poetry was pretentious.

I laughed.

It annoyed me, but it was true.

The same probably could be said in the 21st century about making photographs black and white.

Photographs early on, throughout much of the 19th century, mostly were black and white or sepia and white or variations thereof, depending upon the photographer and the process used. They were that way not because the photographers were pretentious — although they may have been — but because that was all that was available.

When the photographer-chemists first used silver nitrate and other chemicals, they only could produce shades of gray on white. Because this often faded rapidly, some photographers started adding other chemicals to the mix to stabilize the photographs. Chief among these chemicals was sepia, derived from a type of fish. Sepia also had the added benefit of making photos appear warmer, thus playing upon the subconscious of most viewers to see the photos in better mood.

This was the first step, indirectly, toward color photography, but it was a long way off.

And then, when color did arrive for real in the 20th century, the reason people kept shooting black and white film was because color film and color processing was much more expensive.

It wasn't really until the 1970s that color film became the norm and fewer people used black and white. Eventually, this led to black and white film and processing to become rarer and more expensive than color.

Newspapers kept using black and white images long after color was common largely because of the added expense. Black and white photographs only require one plate on the press and one ink. Color photos require four plates and three additional inks.

An odd thing occurred, though, in newspapers. Be-

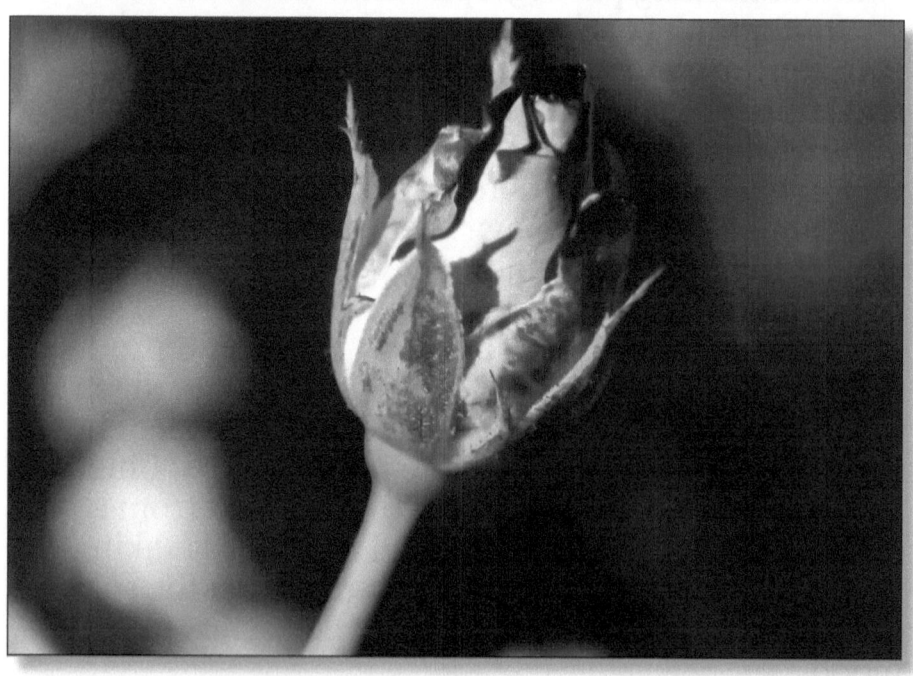

Rose Garden, Central Park, Schenectady, NY, Aug. 17, 2014
Nikon D70, 300mm 1/3200, f/6, ISO 250, Tv, pattern metering
Photo © 2014 by Shawn M. Tomlinson

cause color film and processing were cheaper, many news photographers shot in color. The prints then were rephotographed in black and white with a camera about the size of a third of a room.

It was only after the advent of the harbinger of the end of newspapers — USA Today — that most newspapers went to color.

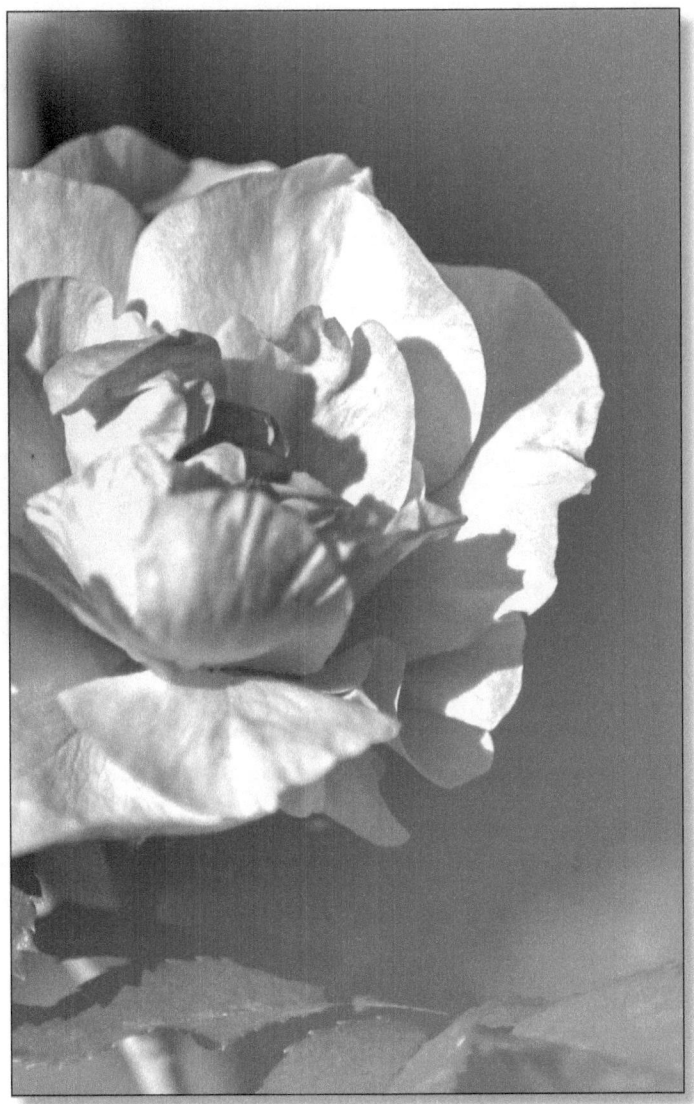

Rose Garden, Central Park, Schenectady, NY, Aug. 17, 2014
Nikon D70, 300mm 1/3200, f/6, ISO 250, Tv, pattern metering
Photo © 2014 by Shawn M. Tomlinson

When digital photography came along, for the pros at least, there still was a reason for black and white. Many newspapers still only could print — or could only afford to print — black and white half-toned

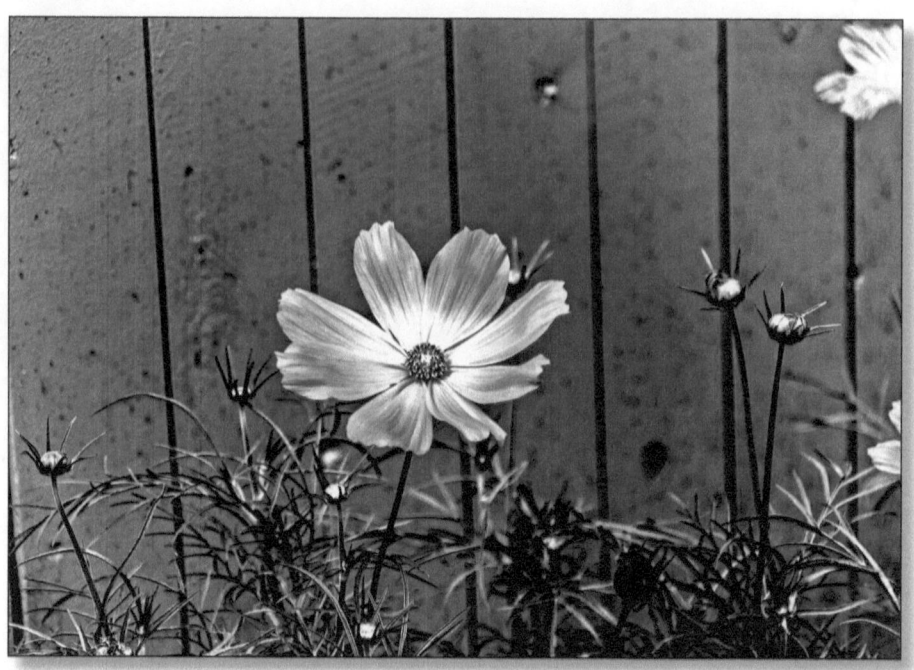

Saratoga Springs, NY, July 1, 2014
Pentax K20D, 200mm, 1/180, f/6.7, ISO 140, Tv, pattern metering
Photo © 2014 by Shawn M. Tomlinson

images. This changed, and black and white images should have died like the pennyfarthing bicycle and the cylinder phonograph.

But it didn't.

Neither did toning, for that matter.

And I'm very glad of that.

In a world dominated by colorful images, black and white and toned photographs can stand out as something different, something somehow more beautiful.

I have a theory as to why this is, a theory I've held for a long time, but somehow it never seemed to catch on.

I still think it's true.

Color is to photographs as TV is to radio.

There, I said it.

OK, what I mean is this.

Back before television was ubiquitous, dramas, comedies, news and sports all were on the radio.

Orson Welles made the world believe he was cowering on a rooftop in New York City while the giant Martian landers destroyed the city around him. He did it while he stood at a microphone and acted from a script held on a sheet music stand in front of him.

The reason people believed it was that Welles was such a brilliant storyteller and that they couldn't see him or the other Radio Mercury Theater on the Air Players. They could only follow the sounds of the voices, sound effects and music.

The rest was filled in by their imaginations.

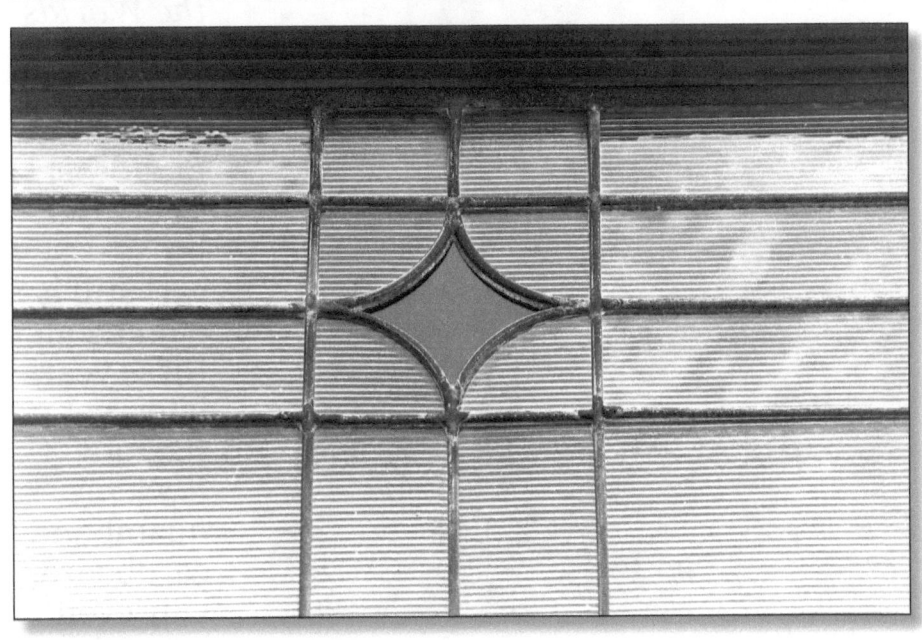

Johnstown, NY, July 25, 2014
Pentax K20D, 200mm, 1/250, f/6.7, ISO 200, Tv, spot metering
Photo © 2014 by Shawn M. Tomlinson

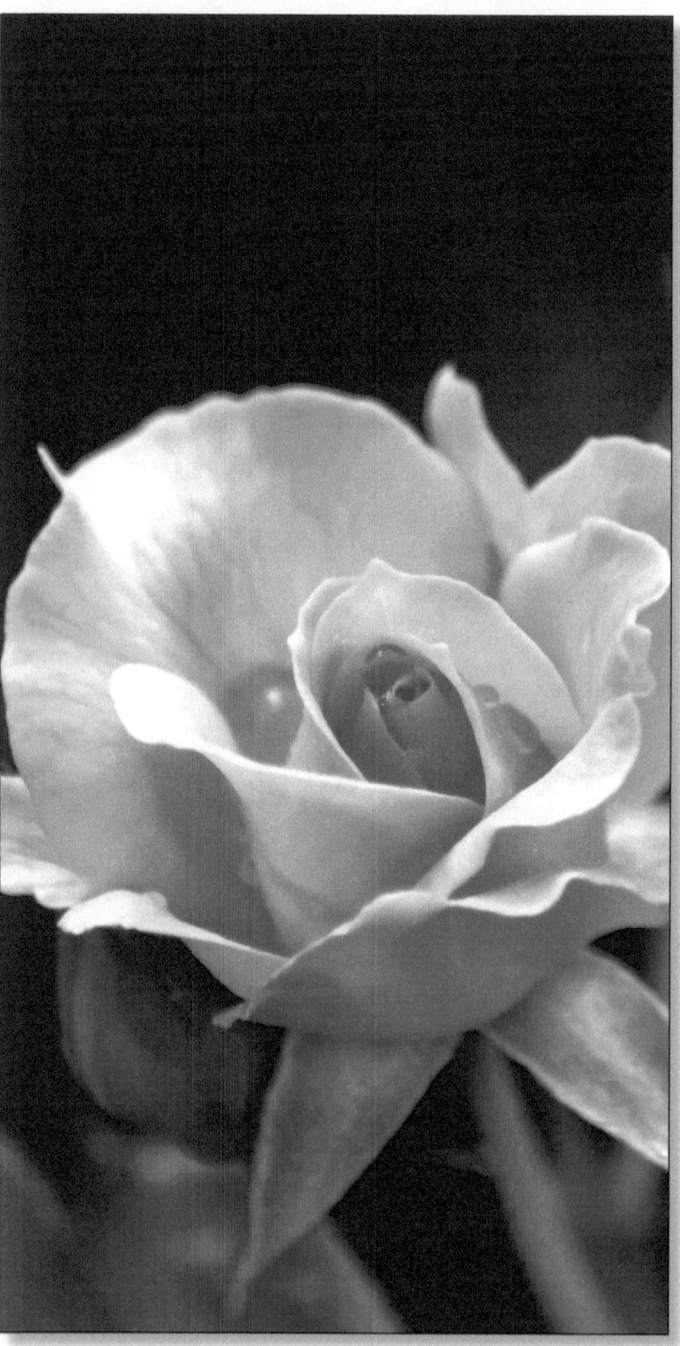

Rose Garden, Central Park, Schenectady, NY, Aug. 17, 2014
Nikon D70, 300mm, 1/1000, f/6, ISO 400, Tv, pattern metering
Photo © 2014 by Shawn M. Tomlinson

Television and film came in and, essentially killed off the imagination in this type of entertainment. Compare the 1953 George Pal-produced film of *War of the Worlds* to Orson Welles' 1938 broadcast. The radio broadcast still is chilling all these years later, yet the movie seems quaint and cardboard, silly even.

And, yes, I

know. Movies already had a long history by the time of Welles' broadcast, but he was smart enough to avoid making a movie of *War of the Worlds* when that's what everyone wanted him to make it. It would have been terrible with 1938 movie technology and techniques.

So he opted to make the greatest movie in history, *Citizen Kane.*

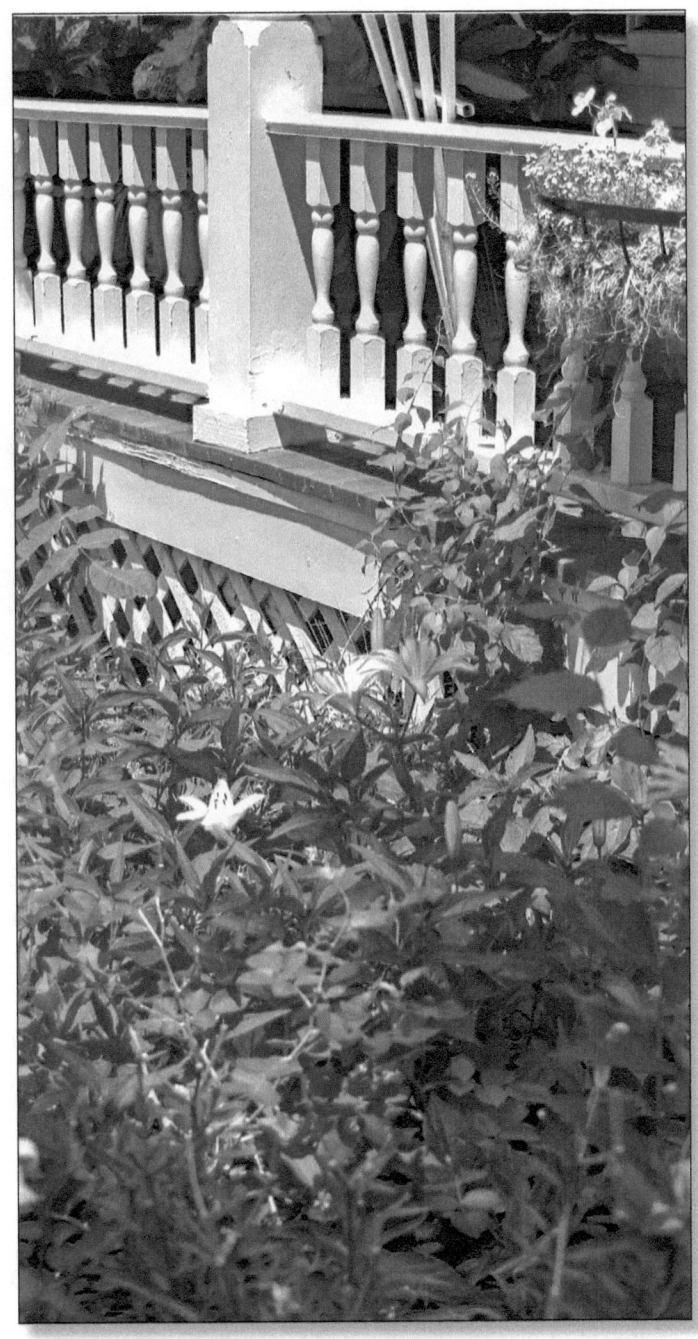

Saratoga Springs, NY, July 1, 2014
Nikon D1, 40mm, 1/640, f/4, ISO 200, Av, pattern metering
Photo © 2014 by Shawn M. Tomlinson

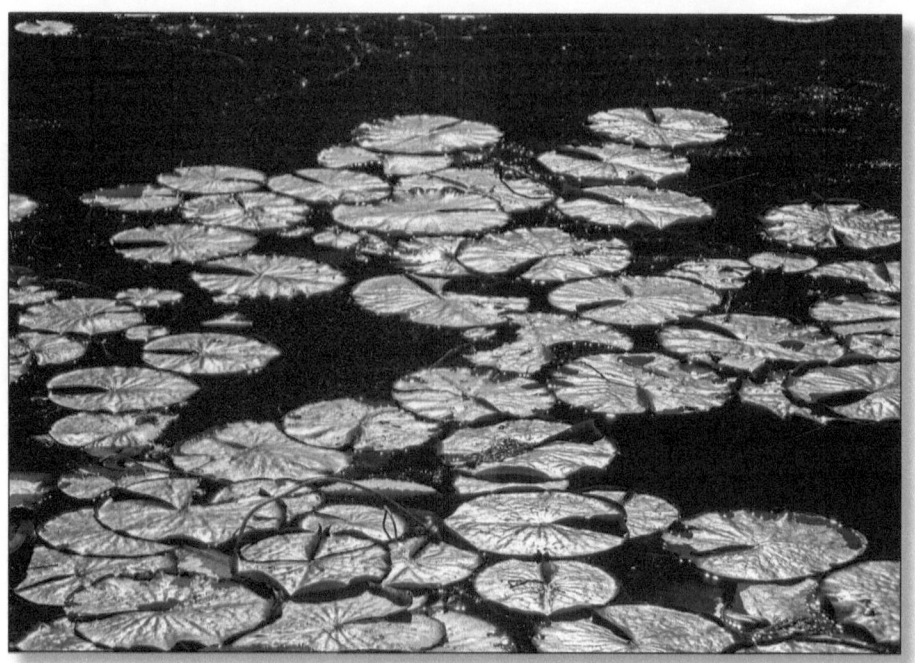

Ballston Lake, NY, July 11, 2014
Canon EOS 20D, 80mm, 1/1600, f/7.1, ISO 200, Tv, pattern metering
Photo © 2014 by Shawn M. Tomlinson

I digress.

The point is that the color visual of the *War of the Worlds* movie as opposed to the radio production, as silly as it is, takes away the imagination element of the story.

When we look at color photographs, we essentially see what are minds tell us is reality. Yes, that rose is red in the photograph because it is red outside my window.

Ho hum.

No imagination needed, thank you.

When we look at the same photograph in black and white or duotoned, it is not the same thing as reality.

It is an extrapolation.

Even though we do not think about it consciously, our minds must put a whole series of things together to make us realize that the black and white image represents a rose, but in a variation of reality.

Neither a color nor a black and white photograph is reality.

Our brains, however, think color photographs are and black and white are not. This sets off a whole process of the imagination, so automatically, we are open to non-real ideas.

OK, so I did not get a $1.2 million grant to study this, and scientists may one day determine I'm wrong, but, hey, it's my theory and I'm stickin' to it.

This theory, I think, goes a long way toward ex-

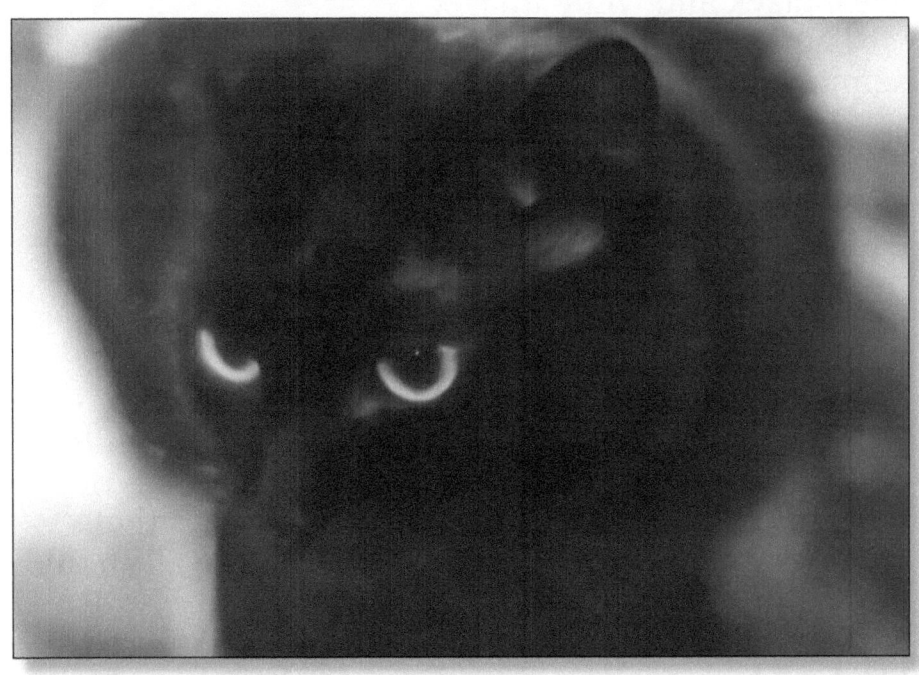

H.P. Lovecraft, Ballston Lake, NY, May 31, 2015.
Nikon D2x, 50mm, 1/40, f/1.8, ISO 1600, Tv, pattern metering
Photo © 2015 by Shawn M. Tomlinson

plaining why we see such drama in black and white images, often the kind of drama we do not see in color photos.

As photographers, though, we must guard against letting ourselves get carried away with this idea and turning everything we shoot in black and white or toned images.

Sure, Adobe Photoshop makes it easy to do this, but that's no reason to do it.

To really work in the 21st century, a black and white or toned image must be special. It must express something not there in color. There must be a reason to change the reality of the image by turning it grayscale, not just that you can.

All that said, there is absolutely nothing like a truly great black and white image.

Think of the stunning work of Ansel Adams in Yosemite and the Southwest.

Or the simple intensity of Imogen Cunningham.

Or the experiments of Alfred Stieglitz that led to photographic standards.

Or Dorothea Lange's stark reality of the Great Depression.

Or the idiosyncratic and brilliant work of Manuel Álvarez Bravo.

The list could go on and does.

These photographers worked in black and white because it was the prime photographic medium of their time. Color film did exists, but it wasn't that good yet and it was expensive and, well, we all should be thankful.

These and many other photographers explored black and white photography. They didn't just shoot. They "saw" in black and white, knew what the colors would translate to, how to use shadow and light.

They "knew" because they learned. They learned by experimenting. The better they got, the more they learned, and the more they can teach.

Not everyone is as good as these photographers, of course, and certainly not every photographer has the same types of vision.

But every photographer has her or his own vision, and it may be different, but it also may be or become brilliant.

This book is intended as a guide to shooting, choosing and editing images as black and white and duotoned images. It certainly does not have all the answers, but it may help you develop your black and white photography skills a bit and launch your new vocation.

— Shawn M. Tomlinson
May 28, 2015
Ballston Lake, NY

Note
Due to printing realities, it is impossible to print duotoned images in the pages of this book. For examples, please see the front and back covers.

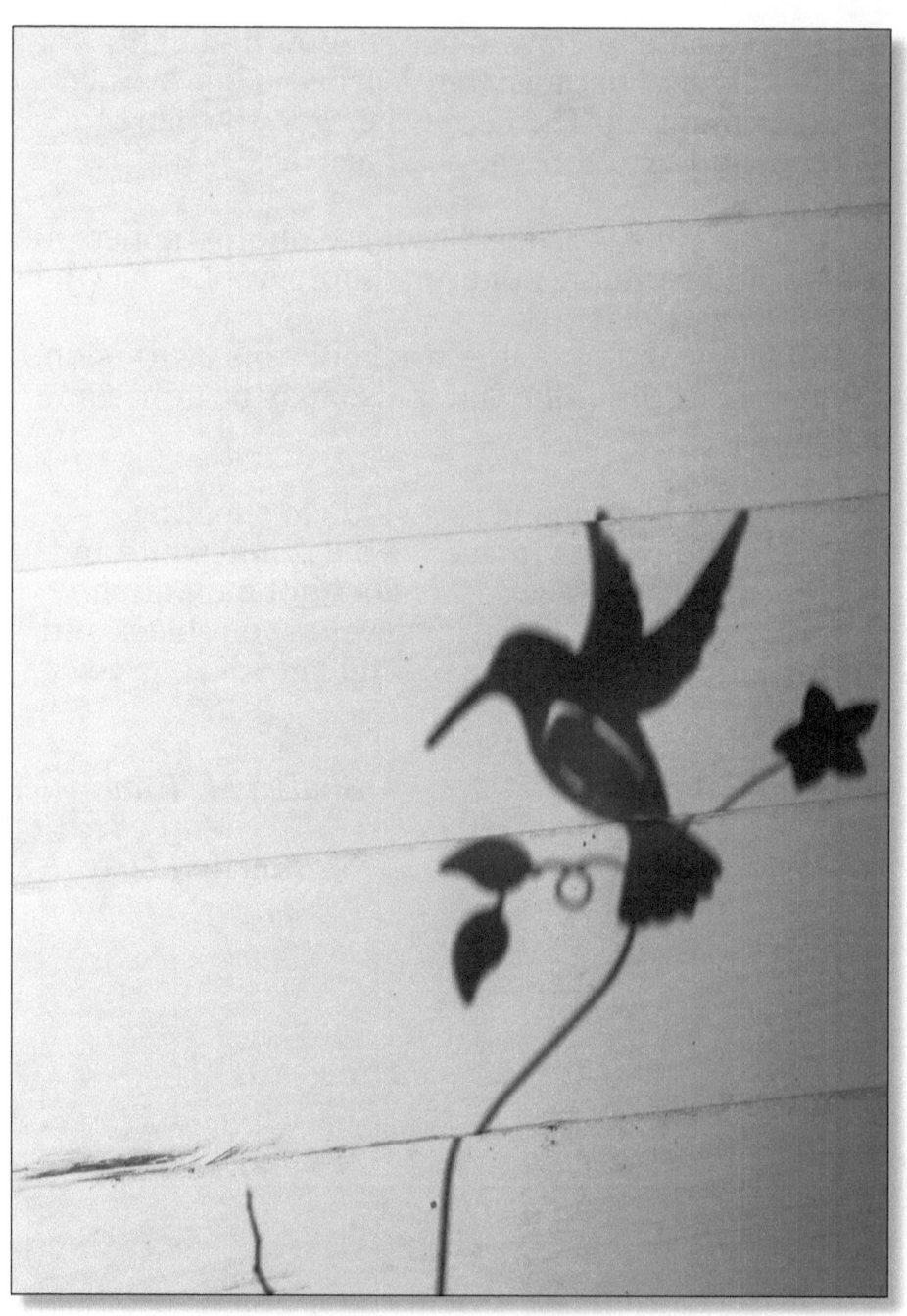

Ballston Lake, NY, Jan. 5, 2015.
Canon EOS 20D, 200mm, 1/500, f/13, ISO 400, Tv, pattern metering
Photo © 2015 by Shawn M. Tomlinson

Part 1:

Basic Concepts

Black and white photographs aren't really black and white.

Make a black and white photocopy of a photograph to see the difference.

Black and white photos actually are made up of 256 shades of gray (Hmmm... I wonder if I could get a best-selling novel with that title?).

Yes, we'll still call them black and white, but I also will refer to them as B&W and grayscale.

I'm not going to go into all the details of how B&W film and prints were made because anyone who would want to know that probably already does.

It is relevant only to film, and this guide is for digital photographers.

That means either photographers shooting with digital single-lens reflex cameras or those shooting with color film, then scanning the negatives/positives. Primarily, though, you are a DSLR photographer and you are working with and uploading digital photo files to your computer to work with in photo editing software.

Some basic assumptions:
• **You ALWAYS and ONLY shoot in RAW.**
• You have a Canon, Nikon or Pentax DSLR. Or Sony or whatever. The brand doesn't matter as much as the DSLR part, but I will be talking in general

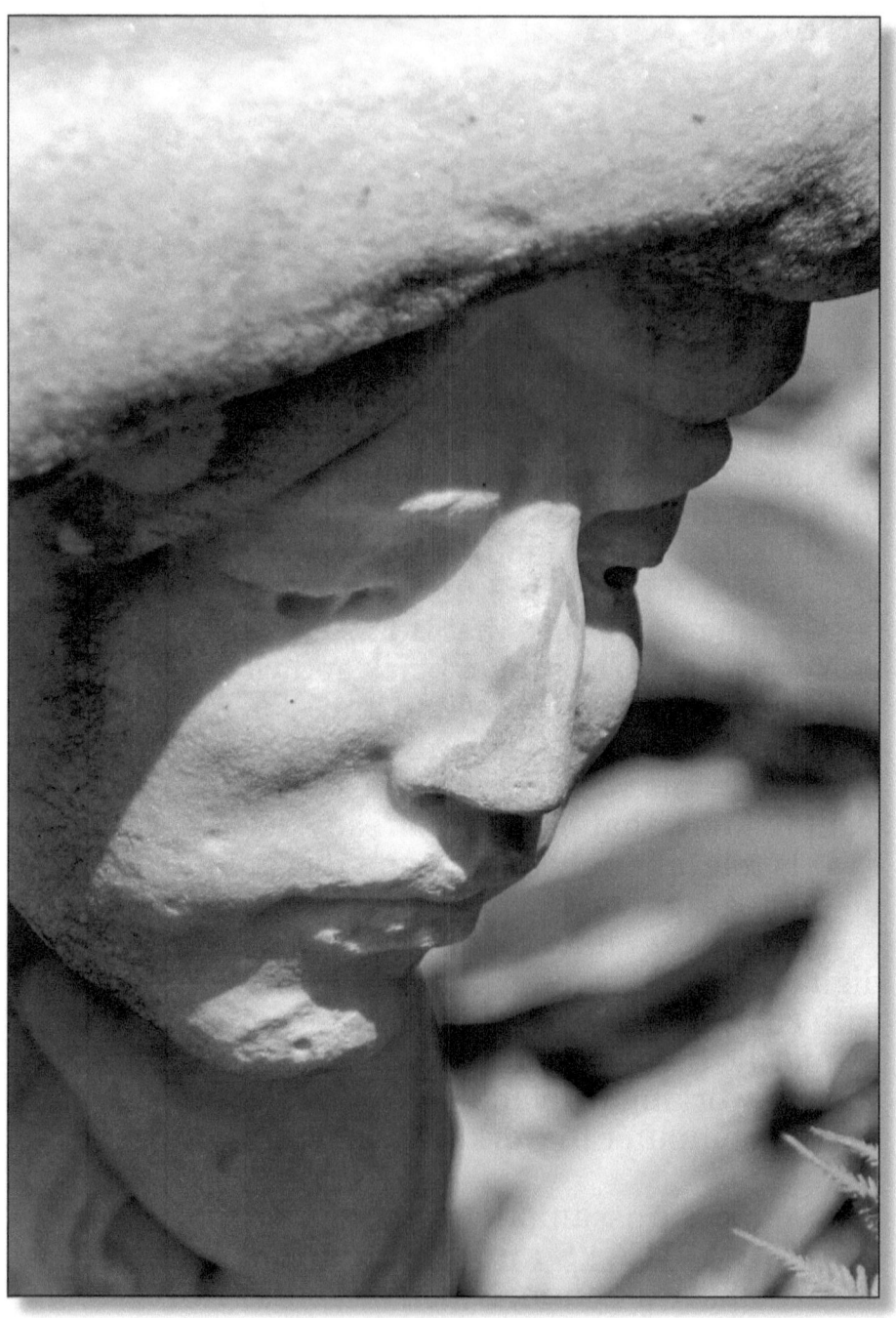

Saratoga Springs, NY, July 1, 2014
Pentax K20D, 200mm, 1/350, f/6.7, ISO 140, Tv, pattern metering
Photo © 2014 by Shawn M. Tomlinson

terms that may use Canon, Nikon and Pentax as examples. The photographs in this book were shot with DSLRs made by these three companies. Yes, I have five working DSLRs, none of them new.

• You will NEVER use your DSLR's built-in B&W mode.

• You are using Adobe Photoshop as your photo editor. Lightroom, Aperture, Gimp and Seashore all do basically the same things, but in different ways.

• You are using an Apple Macintosh computer, or at least are ashamed that you are using a Windows-based computer.

• You have a sense of humor.

The basic tools you need for grayscale photos include:

DSLR
Camera
The DSLR camera is obvious. It is the best tool for most photographers to work with to get the images they want. Nothing against rangefinders (Leica), medium-format (Hasselblad, Pentax, Mamiya, Phase One) or mirrorless (Sony, Nikon, Pentax, etc.), but DSLRs are for serious photographers at any level of skill.

Computer
Obviously, if you are shooting with a DSLR there is no negative/positive piece of plastic film to stick in an enlarger, so you need a computer.

From the comment above, you can tell I prefer Macs. They are better and easier to work with, and that means you won't get bogged down with unnecessary steps that the Windows-based computer requires. The Mac's advantages show through especially with organizing photo files.

Photo editing software

Most people use Adobe Photoshop. Professional photographers often have been lured into the world of Lightroom and Apple's Aperture because the marketing says these programs were designed specifically for the pros. I've used Lightroom and have written about it. I don't like it because of the way it takes over how you organize your photo files. It is very difficult to get around this built-in organizing system, and I have my own system, developed before Lightroom existed.

I hate it when computer programs thing they know

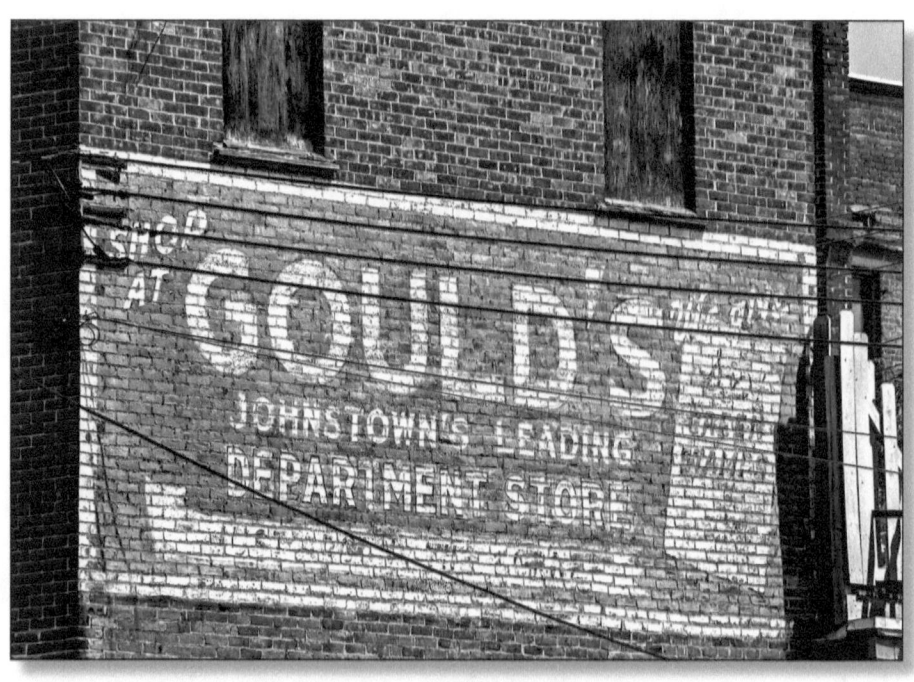

Johnstown, NY, July 25, 2014
Pentax K20D, 200mm, 1/750, f/8, ISO 200, Tv, spot metering
Photo © 2014 by Shawn M. Tomlinson

better than I do.

On the other hand, Lightroom makes great slideshows, far better and simpler than anything else I've seen.

Aperture, of course, like Apple's iPhoto, has been replaced by the combined "Photos" software. Aperture and iPhoto still work on older operating systems.

If you like Aperture or Lightroom, fine. The controls for photo editing are fantastic.

That part I like.

A few tools have different names, but Lightroom's controls are similar to Photoshop.

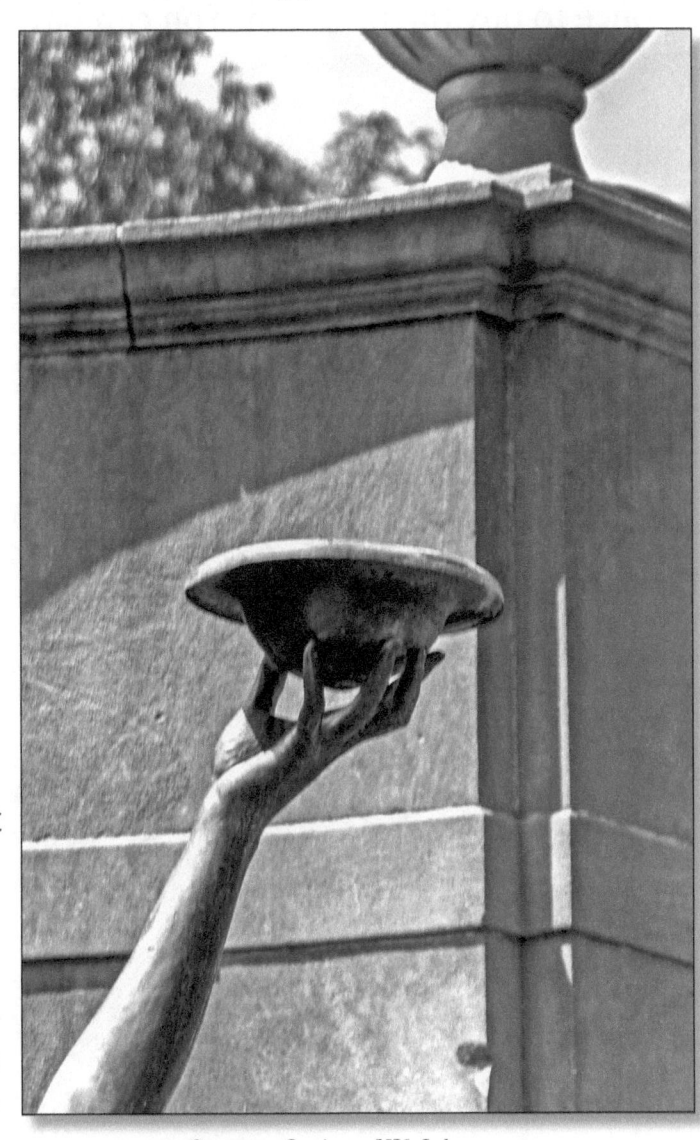

Saratoga Springs, NY, July 1, 2014
Pentax K20D, 200mm, 1/180, f/6.7, ISO 140, Tv, pattern metering
Photo © 2014 by Shawn M. Tomlinson

Adobe, in a move to take complete control of its software, eliminated the boxed programs and now only offers subscriptions. This is the wave of the future. It has some drawbacks, but the main advantage is that you do not have to come up with $700 or $800 at once to buy the program. You can pay monthly for it. Well, you have to, if you want it.

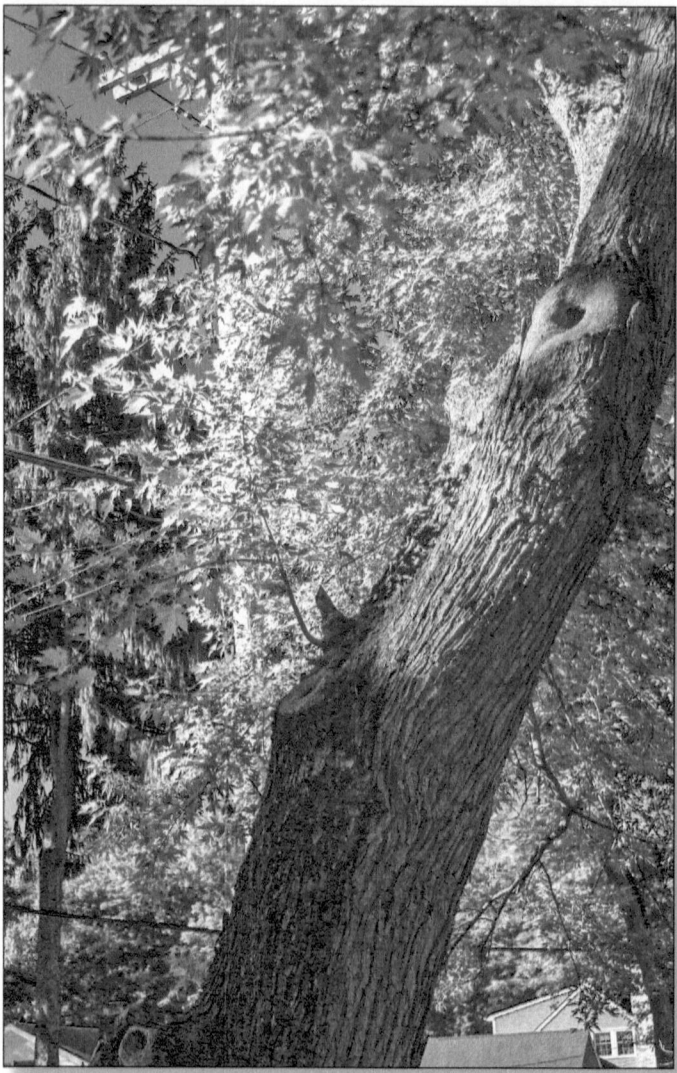

There also are some free photo editing software packages that are quite good. On the Mac (and I think Linux and Windows) Gimp is the most powerful. Seashore is a little more like Adobe's Photoshop Elements but can get the job done.

One of the few drawbacks

Ballston Lake, NY, July 11, 2014
Canon EOS 20D, 42mm, 1/1000, f/4, ISO 200, Tv, pattern metering
Photo © 2014 by Shawn M. Tomlinson

of Macs is the iPhoto software, but as mentioned, it has been discontinued. It was fine for amateurs shooting with smartphones, but its limitations could be terribly frustrating to photographers. I recommend against using it for anything. Well, except for slideshows. It did an OK job creating slideshows of your images, but it required fixing them to your taste in another application before importing them to iPhoto for your slideshows.

B&W printer (if you intend to print your images)

This is a tough one, and other than your DSLR and lenses, the most expensive thing you'll need.

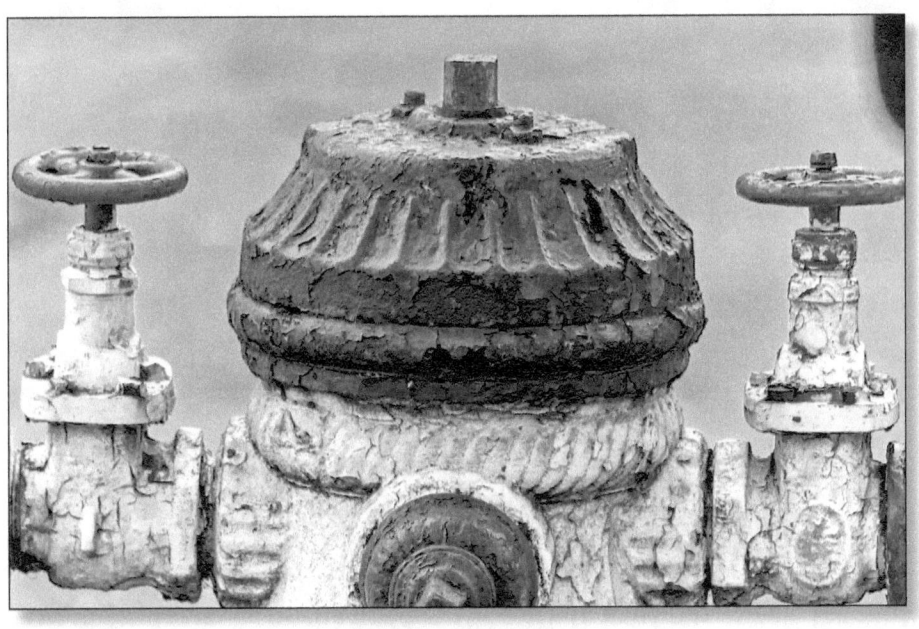

Saratoga Springs, NY, Aug. 23, 2014
Nikon D70, 180mm, 1/800, f/4.8, ISO 400, Tv, pattern metering
Photo © 2014 by Shawn M. Tomlinson

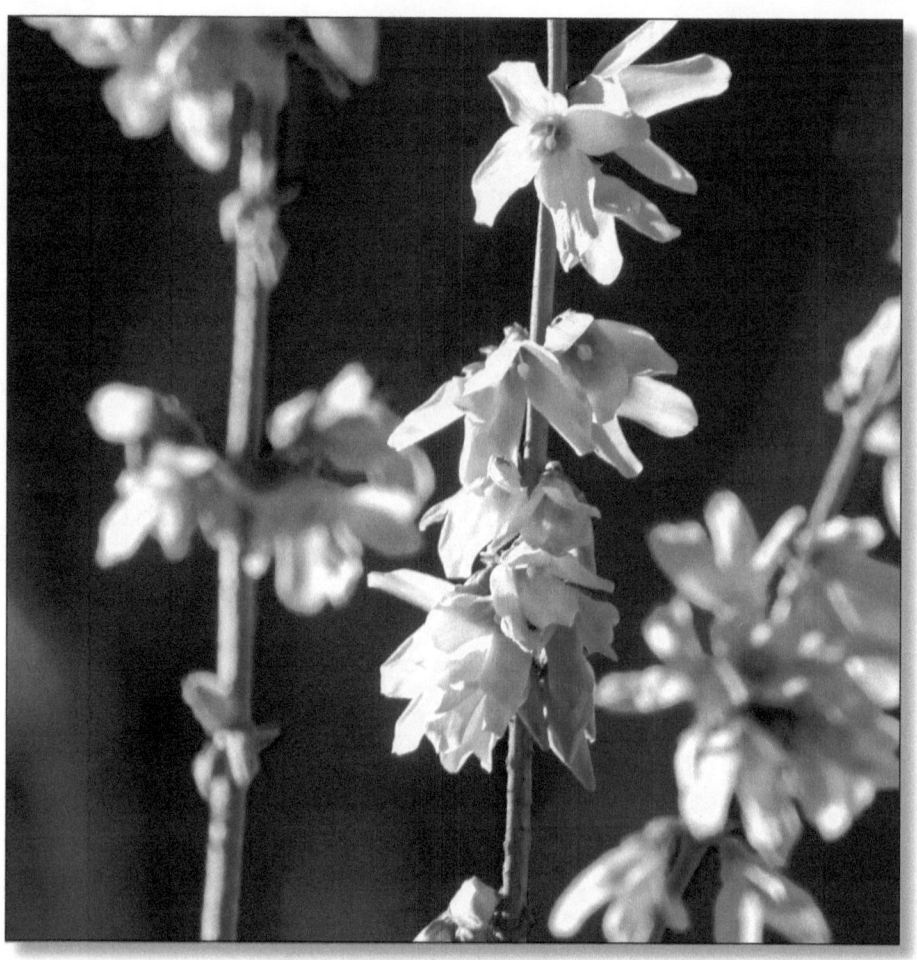

Ballston Lake, NY, April 18, 2015.
Nikon D2x, 300mm, 1/250, f/11, ISO 250, Tv, pattern metering
Photo © 2015 by Shawn M. Tomlinson

Regular ink jet printers are fine for color images, although as a photographer, you probably will want something more than the $100 all-in-one variety.

But when it comes to grayscale images, regular cheap printers just don't do a good job.

The reason is that these types of printers blend the CMYK colors — cyan, magenta, yellow and black ("K" stands for registration from the newspaper days, and registration is black) — to make the shades of gray required for B&W photos. This often means that you will not get true blacks, and your prints may have color casts over them, such as green or blue.

If you are serious about printing a lot of your images in high-quality grayscale, you will need a grayscale printer.

Printers come and go rapidly, but the Epson R2400 was the standard grayscale printer for photographers for several years. The company has replaced it, and the closet thing to it now costs as much as a mid-range DSLR, not to mention the quite high cost for Epson ink. The current as of 2014 Epson with "Advanced Black-and-White Photo Mode" is the Stylus Pro 3880.

Canon also makes good printers. I had a little one for years that made really good photo prints, but not quite to professional levels. The current Canon Pixma Pro-1 is comparable to the Epson and costs about the same.

Both of these printers work on Macs and PCs, but not all Canon printers do. They used to, but some of the slightly lower models appear to be only compatible with Windows-based computers, so these obviously are not meant for serious photographers.

Also keep in mind that, as a photographer, you most likely will be printing your photos bigger than 8.5-by-11, so when considering a printer, make sure it handles bigger paper sizes. The two mentioned here do.

If you only intend your images for electronic display, you won't need a printer, but that seems a waste. It prevents you from exhibiting your images in a gallery, which you may want to do.

Of course, you can have a lab print your images, and the technicians there most likely will create better prints than you could at home.

Except that you won't be there when they print them, so you will have no control over them.

Prints, by the way, rarely look the same as the images you see on your computer display. There are two reasons.

First, the images are backlit on your display, and that always improves image quality.

Second, your printer and your display rarely are calibrated to the same specifications. You can work to fix this by calibrating your display — and you should — but that doesn't solve the problem completely.

Like Ansel Adams dancing around his darkroom dodging and burning to get the perfect print, you will have to experiment and work to get the prints you want.

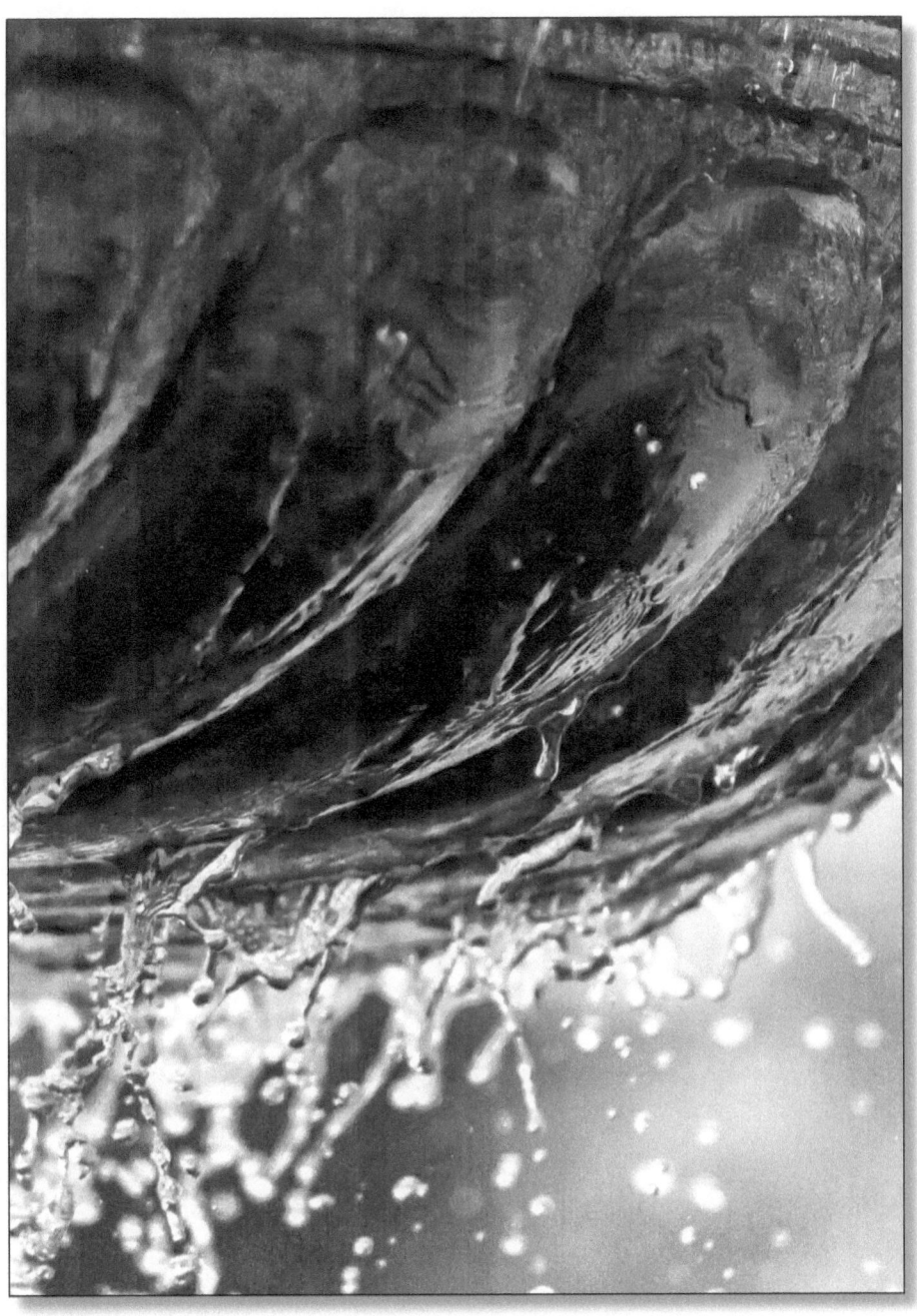

Rose Garden, Central Park, Schenectady, NY, Aug. 17, 2014
Nikon D70, 300mm, 1/3200, f/6, ISO 250, Tv, pattern metering
Photo © 2014 by Shawn M. Tomlinson

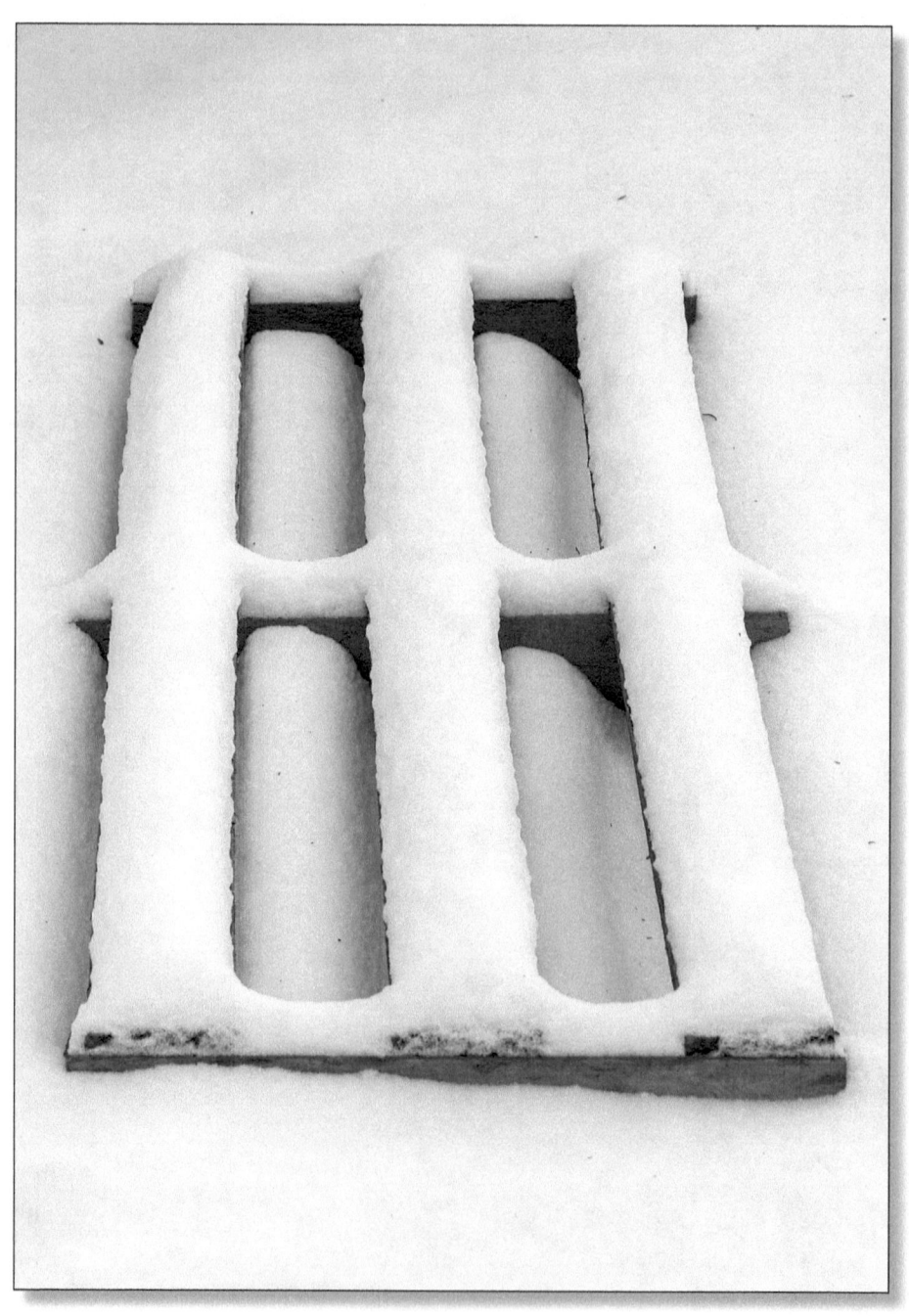

Ballston Lake, NY, Jan. 9, 2015.
Canon EOS 20D, 50mm, 1/1000, f/6.3, ISO 200, Tv, pattern metering
Photo © 2015 by Shawn M. Tomlinson

Part 2:

Never Shoot in B&W With a DSLR

OK, most DSLR cameras these days have a built-in black and white mode that lets you shoot in, well, black and white.

Don't use it.

Experiment with it if you like, but don't use it for serious work.

You won't be able to anyway, if you follow **THE RULES** and **ONLY SHOOT IN RAW**.

I didn't realize this at first.

I decided to experiment with my Canon EOS 20D just for the hell of it. I tried some of the effects, particularly the infrared setting, and things looked great on the Canon's LCD. I was just experimenting, so I didn't care that no color images would be recorded.

The thing is, they were.

I **ALWAYS shoot in RAW** as you should.

When I uploaded the B&W images to the Mac Pro, I opened Adobe Bridge to that folder.

Bridge does this thing where it has extra dark black borders around the thumbnail images to tell you that the thumbnails have not yet been fully rendered. As Bridge renders each image, it gets clearer and these black borders disappear.

I'm used to this. I let Bridge do its thing because

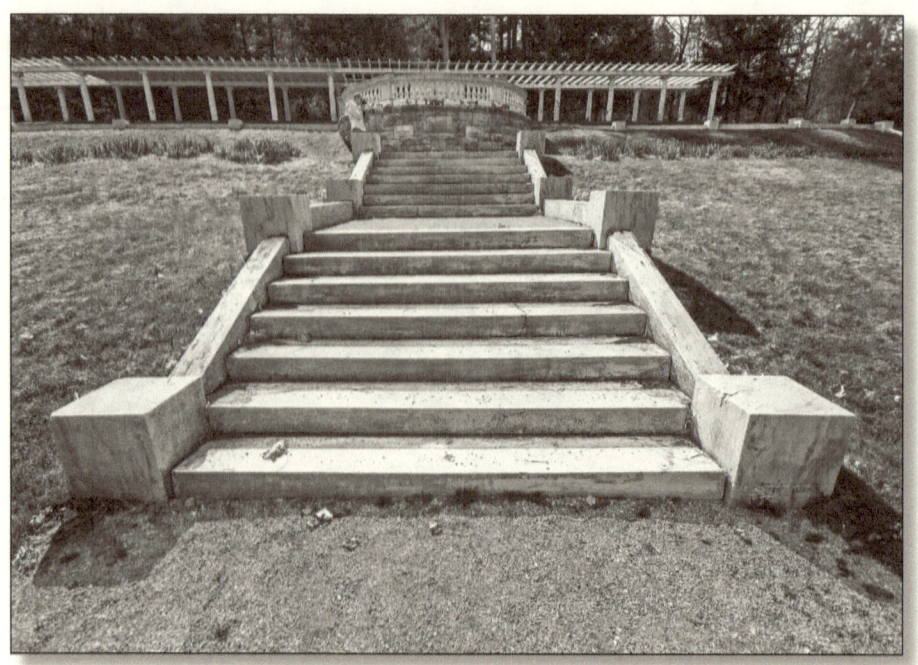

Gary Ziroli, Yaddo, Saratoga Springs, NY, April 18, 2015.
Nikon D2x, 10mm, 1/800, f/6, ISO 250, Tv, pattern metering
Photo © 2015 by Shawn M. Tomlinson

when it's done, I can select all the images, open File Info, and input the global details of that photo shoot. I do this before I touch a single image because, shooting every day as I do, it would be easy to forget where each image was taken and under what circumstances. By doing it at the start, the data is copied over to the edited TIFF image file. I can go back and add things such as people in the photos or whatever.

So, as I watched Bridge render the thumbnails, they all changed one by one from black and white to color. I was confounded. I'm not sure why this happens, except that because the files are RAW data, they are recorded with all the information from the second the shutter button is pressed.

Which means they are in color.

The 20D's B&W mode is only a filter, layered on top of the RAW data. I have not tried it, but I'm guessing that if I shot in JPEG, the images would be recorded only in grayscale.

And, of course, shooting in JPEG is a **BAD THING** for photographers. It saves memory card and hard drive

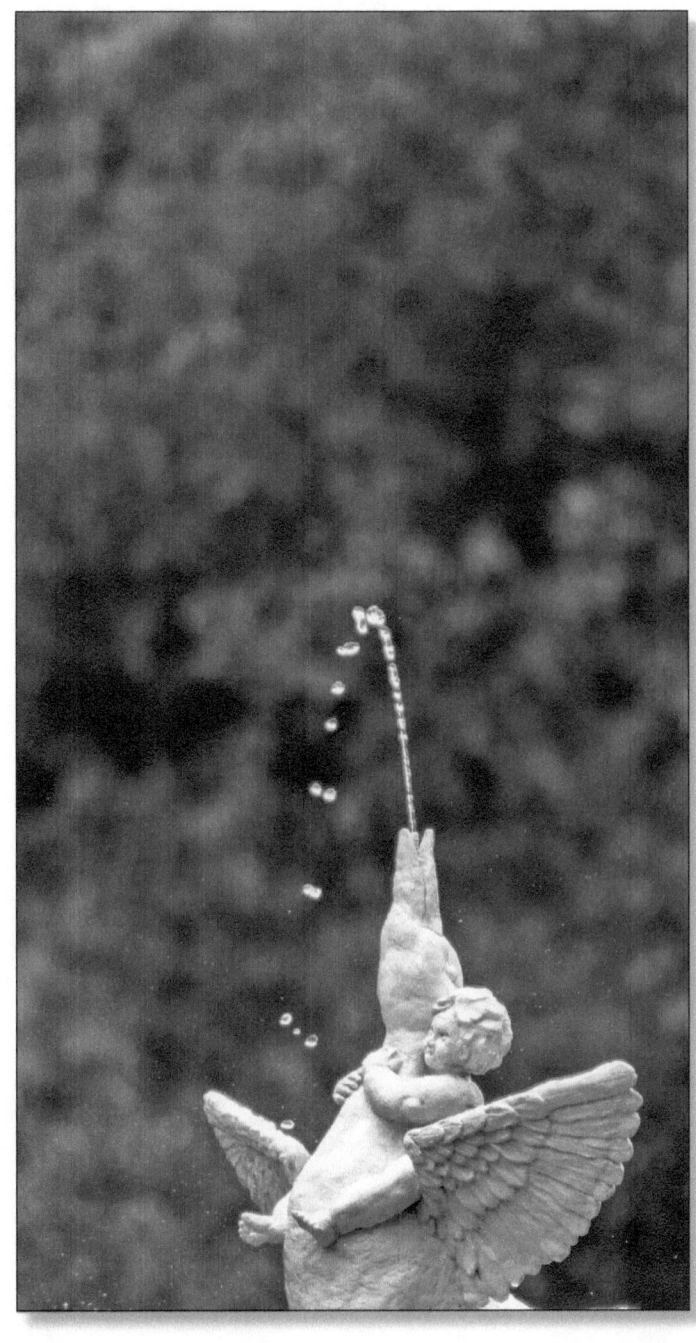

Congress Park, Saratoga Springs, NY, Aug. 23, 2014
Nikon D70, 300mm, 1/1000, f/6, ISO 400, Tv, pattern metering
Photo © 2014 by Shawn M. Tomlinson

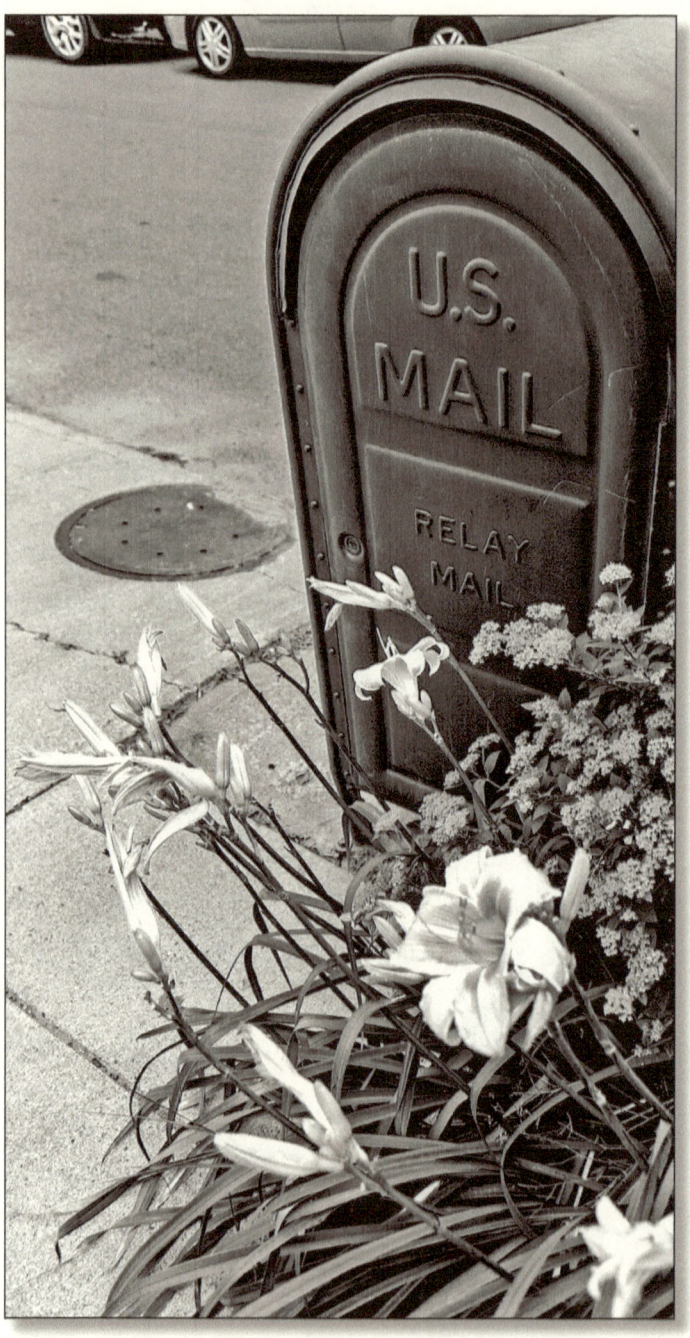

space, but severely limits what you can do with your images. To me, shooting images in JPEG makes them appear flat and lifeless. I've done it by accident a few times when turning the Mode Dial. Instead of going to Aperture-Priority Mode from Shutter-Priority Mode or to Manual Mode, I've slipped and pushed the Mode dial too far to the Auto Mode,

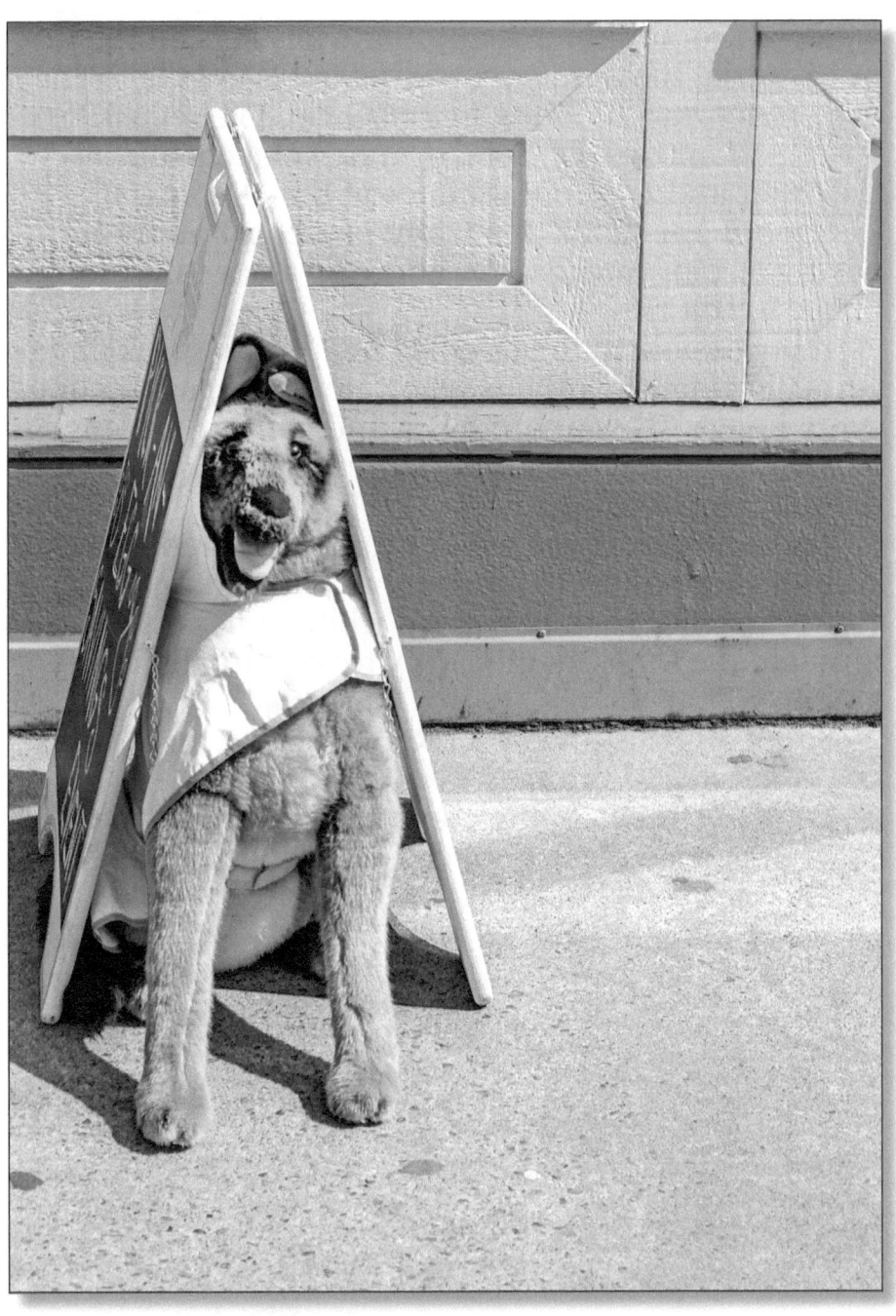

Saratoga Springs, NY, April 4, 2015.
Nikon D7000, 50mm, 1/800, f/5.6, ISO 100, Tv, pattern metering
Photo © 2015 by Shawn M. Tomlinson

which on some cameras automatically sets all the input criteria, including overriding my RAW file format preference and shooting in JPEG. So, I've seen JPEG and RAW images shot of the same subjects one after the other and I simply shudder at the JPEGs.

Shooting in black and white prevents you from having a color image later, and your image may look better in color.

It is possible to turn a color image into black and white, but not the other way around. And, again, not every image will work in black and white. Sure, it will be a photograph, but it may suffer dramatically from the removal of color.

For example, if you shoot brightly colored autumn scenes, they will have much more effect upon the viewer in color than black and white, unless you manipulate the tones significantly to an unrealistic degree.

Shoot all your images in RAW without any of the DSLR's "effects" filters.

You have much better tools for converting your color images to black and white in Photoshop than in your camera.

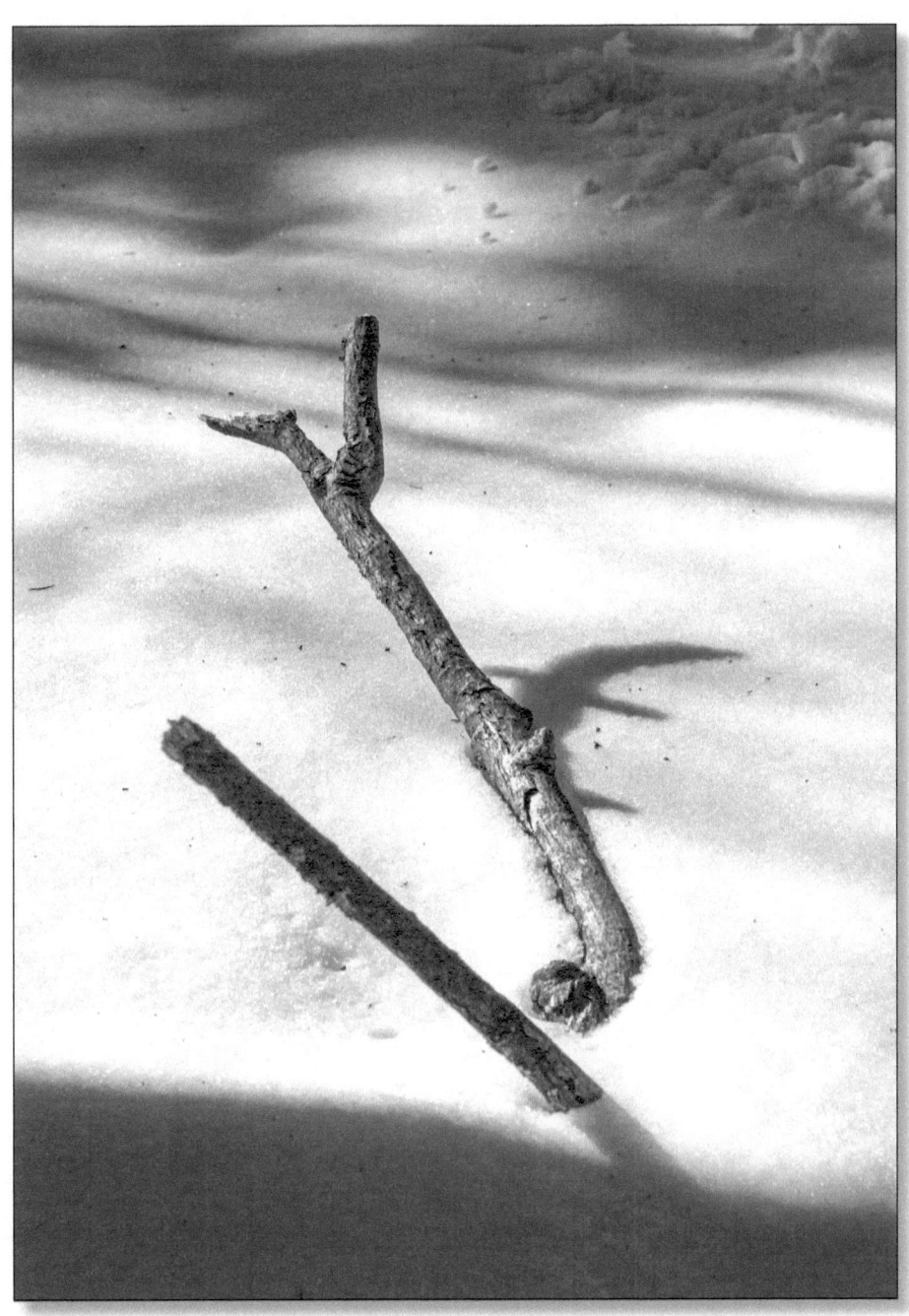

Ballston Lake, NY, March 6, 2015.
Sony A100, 50mm, 1/4000, f/6.3, ISO 400, Tv, pattern metering
Photo © 2015 by Shawn M. Tomlinson

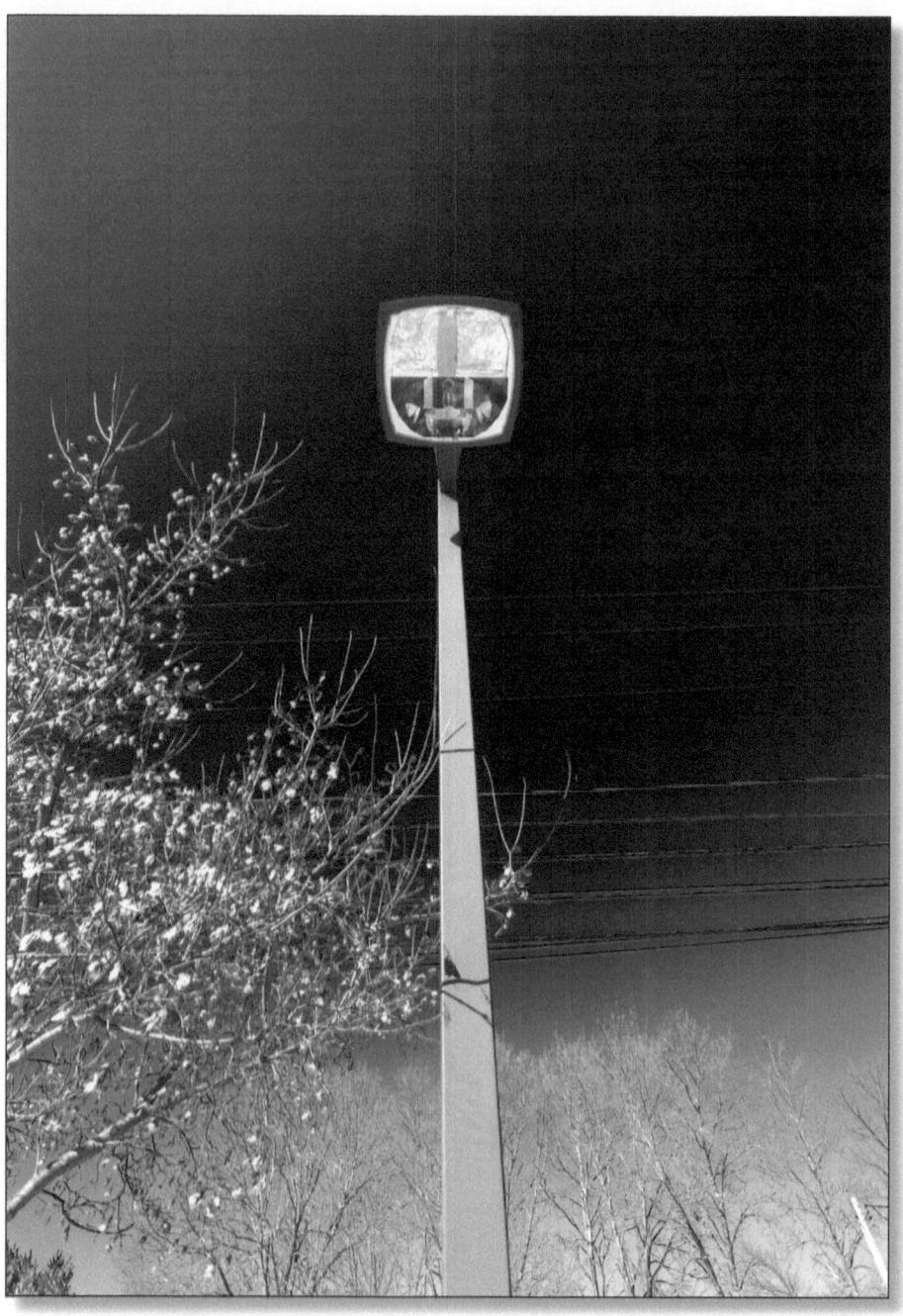

Ballston Lake, NY, March 23, 2015.
Nikon D2x, 11mm, 1/1000, f/4.2, ISO 250, Tv, pattern metering
Photo © 2015 by Shawn M. Tomlinson

Part 3:

Learning to See

The easiest way to create B&W photographs is to just shoot normally, then try each image in your photo editing software as a grayscale image.

I admit to doing this sometimes, and you probably will do it, too, but, as you learn to "see" in black and white, this task will take less time.

What I mean by "seeing" in black and white is that, once you are used to how colors translate to grayscale, you will begin to recognize scenes that will work particularly well in the latter format.

As I said, I've been shooting B&W images since the film days of the mid-1970s. The problem for me was that there was a long gap of years between the time I shot mostly in B&W and when I went back to doing it. By then, everything had changed.

I was working as the Sunday editor at a newspaper that had, a year of two earlier, made the transition to digital photography. As cheap as the powers that be at this company were, somehow someone convinced them that they should lay out $6,000 for a Nikon D1. That is the first DSLR I used with a quick lesson from the photographer and from a sports editor who knew the camera better.

Of course, everything was in color, but except for the front, inside front, inside back and back pages, everything else was in black and white. That meant I

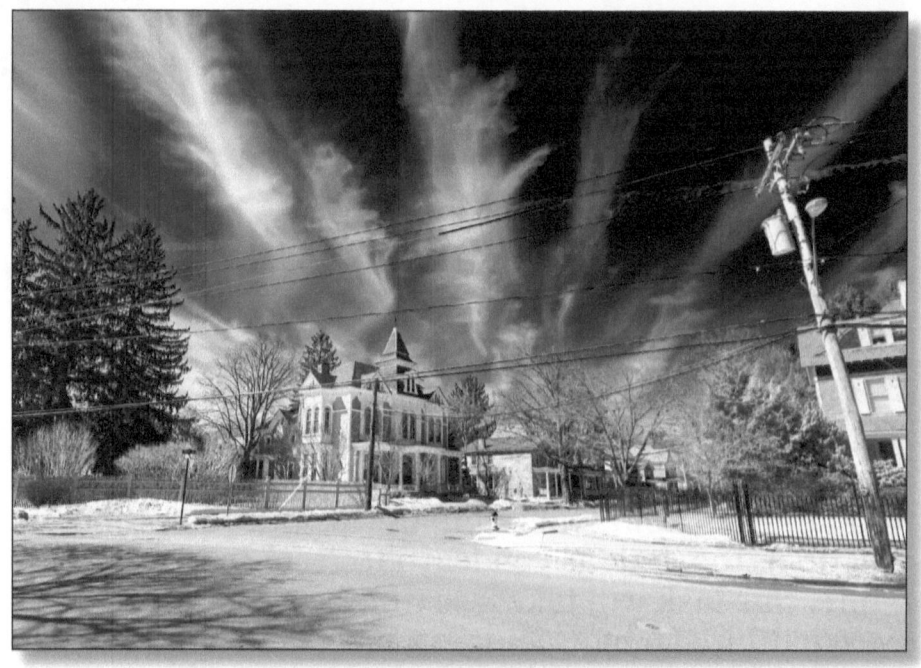

Saratoga Springs, NY, March 24, 2015.
Nikon D7000, 10mm, 1/1250, f/6.3, ISO 250, Tv, pattern metering
Photo © 2015 by Shawn M. Tomlinson

had to convert all the images, and that's where I realized I needed to relearn what I had once known.

See, with an enlarger, it was possible to make B&W prints from color negatives, but they tended to print flat and with a lack of dynamics or "umph!" Kodak did make a photo paper — Panalure: "This is a panchromatic, resin-coated, developer incorporated, projection-speed paper designed for making black-and-white enlargements (or contact prints with reduced illumination) from color negatives"* — but to my eye, the prints still lacked the contrast and dynamic I

---

* — Quoted from the data sheet titled, "Technical Data/Black and White Paper: June 2005 • G-27: Kodak Professional Panalure Select RC Paper. http://www.kodak.com/global/en/professional/support/techPubs/g27/g27.pdf

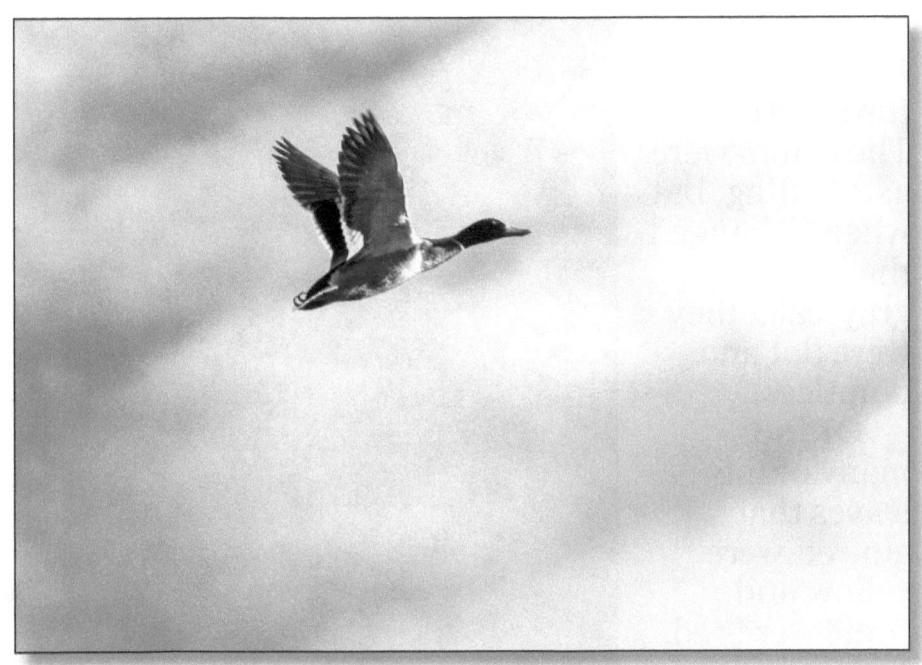

Glenville, NY, March 27, 2015.
Nikon D7000, 300mm, 1/500, f/8, ISO 250, Tv, pattern metering
Photo © 2015 by Shawn M. Tomlinson

wanted.

So, imagine my joy at discovering that Adobe Photoshop allowed me to create really good B&W images from color photos.

At the time, Photoshop still was a little primitive, but it worked much better than B&W prints from color negatives in an enlarger, even from color negatives scanned.

Once Adobe introduced a tool under Adjustments that allowed for even more control over B&W images, well, it became possible for anyone to do it.

So, as I indicated, I really discovered how to use this tool — simply called Black & White under Image>Adjustments — after shooting many autumn photos at the Indian Kill Nature Preserve. The colors were astounding, but when I changed the images to grayscale, they were flat and pointless.

OK, so, many of the leaves that glowed were yellow and some were red. In grayscale, well, they were uniformly gray.

Using the Black & White tool with its Yellow and Red sliders, I was able to bring back the dynamic of the original images in grayscale.

Aside from learning how to use the Adobe tool, this also started or restarted me

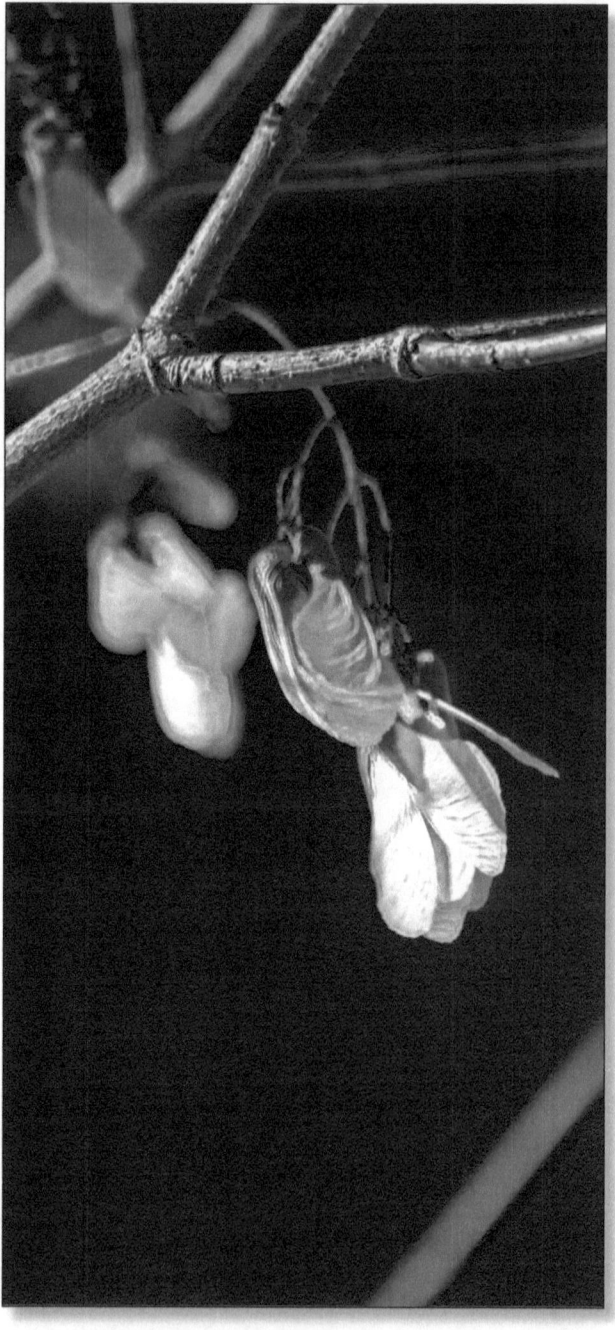

Ballston Lake, NY, March 9, 2015.
Nikon D2x, 300mm, 1/1250, f/5.6, ISO 200, Tv, pattern metering
Photo © 2015 by Shawn M. Tomlinson

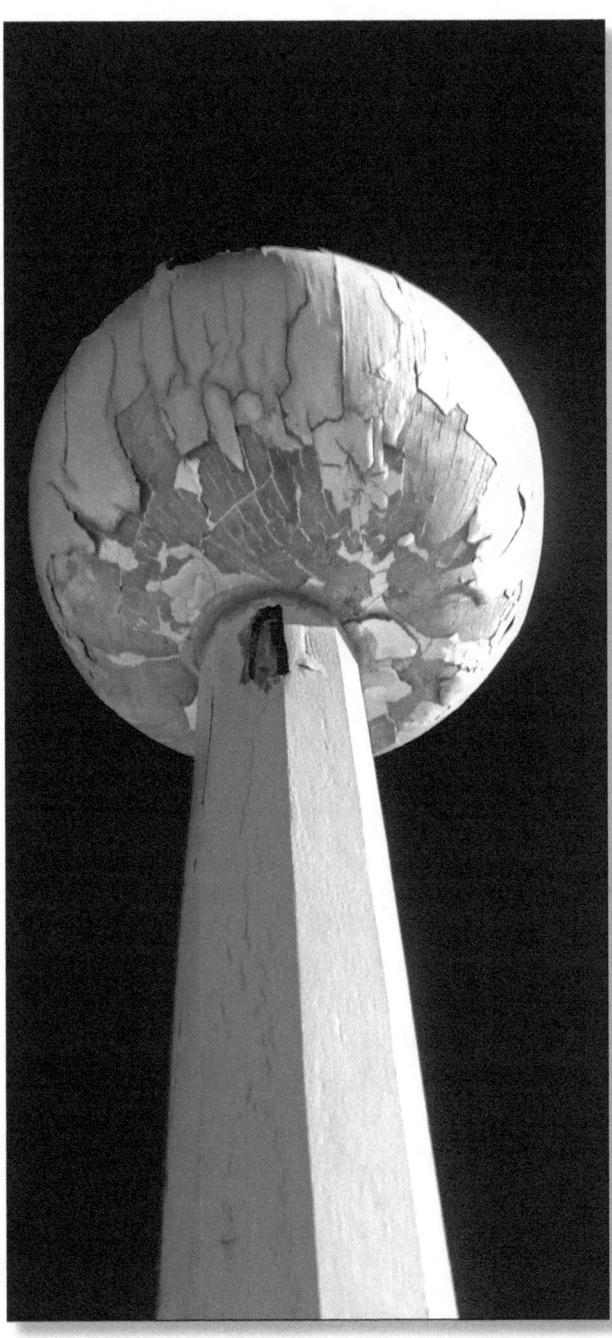

Ballston Spa, NY, March 11, 2015.
Nikon D2x, 270mm, 1/1000, f/5.3, ISO 400, Tv, pattern metering
Photo © 2015 by Shawn M. Tomlinson

thinking about B&W in the colorful world.

I started to teach myself again how to "see" what colors would do in black and white.

Unless you have a natural talent for it, the best way to do this is to look at many of the photographs you take, convert them to black and white using the correct tools and see what works for you.

To make this work faster, return to the same place multiple times as you learn more and shoot the same types of scenes, but with an eye to what will work

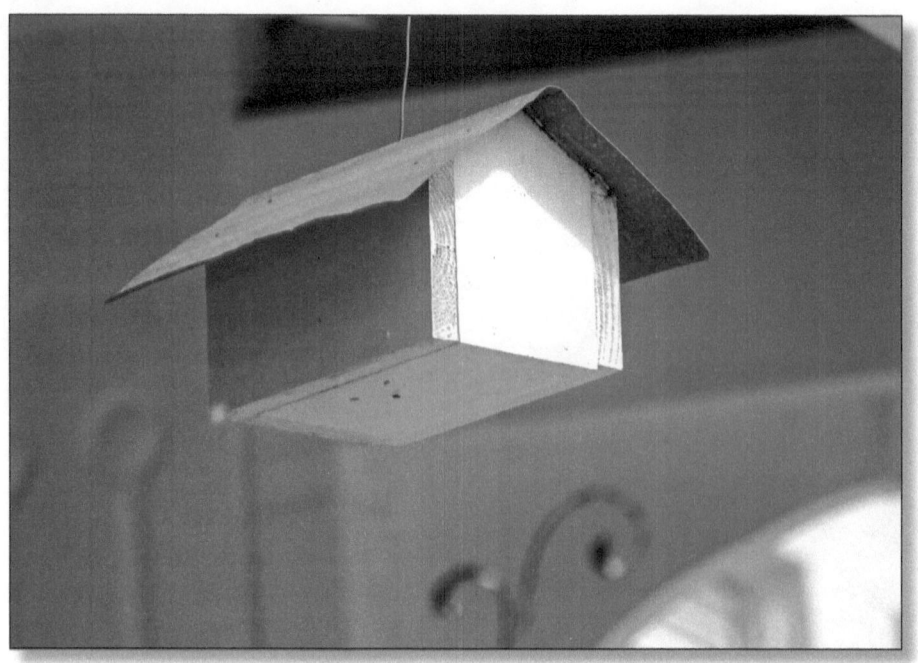

Saratoga Springs, NY, March 28, 2015.
Nikon D7000, 300mm, 1/800, f/5.6, ISO 250, Tv, pattern metering
Photo © 2015 by Shawn M. Tomlinson

in B&W.

Sometimes, you will find that something you think will work great in grayscale, simply does not.

It's OK.

Don't worry about it and move on.

Sometimes, the opposite will happen.

The best example of this I can give you was my trip to the Rose Garden in Central Park in Schenectady, N.Y.

Rose Garden, right?

Brightly colored roses, right?

And, of course, that's true. The images I shot that day — more than 500 — have great color and really, ahem excuse me, "pop."

I should mention here — and elsewhere in this book — that these images were made with the consumer-level and by then quite old Nikon D70 with its 6.1 megapixels. I paid less than $100 for that wonderful camera from a used market seller. To top that off, they all were shot with a low-end Tamron 70-300mm lens for which, I am not kidding, I paid $29.

It is true that the 6.1-megapixel D70 will not reproduce the detail that, say, the Nikon D810 with its 36 megapixels will. And that Tamron lens with the bad chromatic aberrations produces somewhat soft images.

In this case, that worked in my favor.

The softer nature of the images really showed the

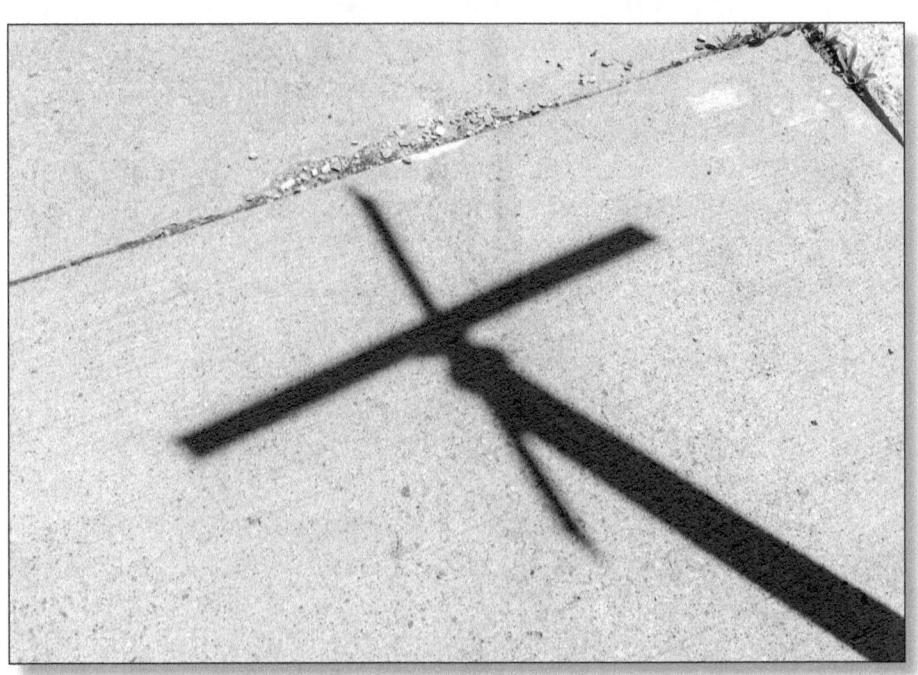

Saratoga Springs, NY, June 6, 2015.
Nikon D7000, 35mm, 1/500, f/11, ISO 200, P, spot metering
Photo © 2015 by Shawn M. Tomlinson

beauty of the flowers.

I've also gotten amazingly colorful flower images with my ancient Nikon D1 at 2.65 megapixels with the same lens.

The point is, you really don't need high resolution and the best lens to create great images. Better DSLRs and better lenses will produce sharper images, but that's not always what I want.

Sometimes, however, having a newer camera with a much better lens is essential.

Today, for example, I shot the same lilacs with the aforementioned Tamron lens on the 12-megapixels Nikon D2x and then with the Nikon AF D 50mm f/1.8 lens on the 16.7-megapixel Nikon D7000. There was no question that the images hot with the latter combination were better, certainly much sharper.

Prime or fixed focal length lenses — as opposed to zooms — always produce sharper images.

So, why to I continue to use that old Tamron? Well, it has macro capability and at 300mm the bokeh is fantastic. Bokeh is a Japanese word meaning blur. In photography, it means you have a nicely blurred background with a sharp central subject.

Anyway, when I got home and started looking at the Rose Garden images, I was very pleased and slightly surprised. I went to the Rose Garden on a whim that warm, sunny day in August, and I could have taken my then-highest-resolution DSLR, the Pentax K20D at 14 megapixels.

I chose the D70 because I had just gotten it as a replacement for one that didn't work quite right and I was eager to shoot with it.

So, sure, I was quite pleased with the color images. They were and are some of the best I've ever shot.

Then, for some reason, I decided to try some of

them in black and white, and then in duotone.

Then, I really had to say "wow" as my eyes widened.

Some of these images are included in this book, and there is one on the front cover as well as another on the back cover.

This episode taught me an entirely new way to look at flowers, and well, everything else.

It taught me how to really

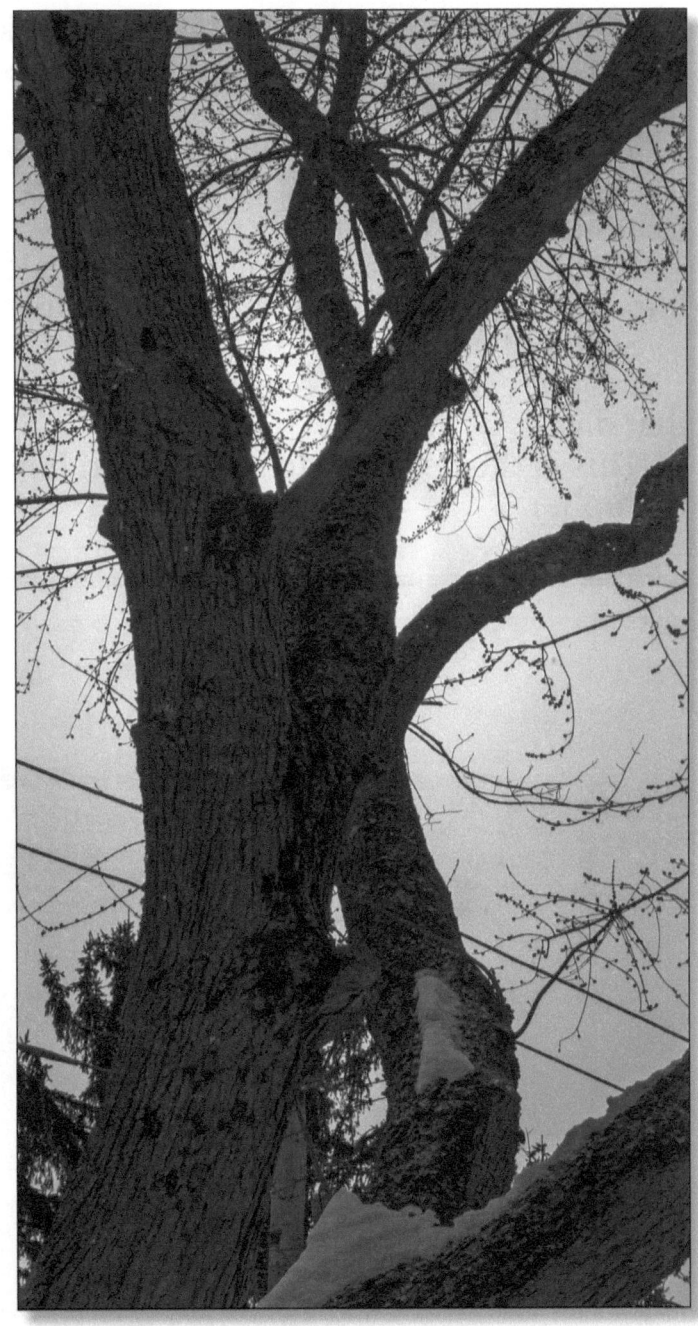

Ballston Lake, NY, March 1, 2015.
Canon EOS 20D, 50mm, 1/2000, f/11, ISO 400, P, pattern metering
Photo © 2015 by Shawn M. Tomlinson

"see" in black and white, and to use that knowledge to capture images that I specifically intended to convert to grayscale.

This isn't so much something that can be taught as it is something that must be learned through experimentation.

Remember that shooting digital images, unlike on film, costs nothing more the more images you shoot.

So shoot a lot.

I shoot every day, no matter what else I must do that day.

This is the best way to really learn how to be a photographer.

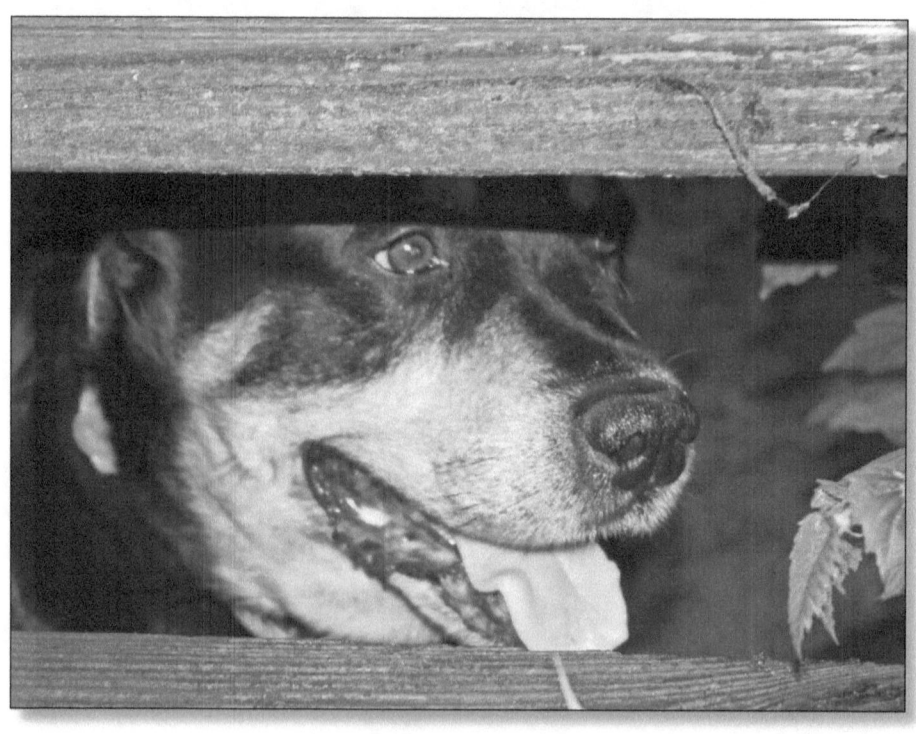

Baby, Ballston Lake, NY, June 14, 2013.
Pentax K20D, 55mm, 1/60, f/5.6, ISO 200, P, spot metering
Photo © 2013, 2015 by Shawn M. Tomlinson

Part 4:
Selecting Subjects

Some subjects work better in black and white, but that may not be obvious until you are seeing them in Adobe Photoshop.

However, when you have converted enough photographs to good black and white images, you will begin to understand what works and what won't out when you are out in the field.

I started shooting on black and white film in the mid-1970s because it was cheaper, I could develop it myself and it seemed more dramatic to my teenage sensibilities. So I have many years of experience "seeing" black and white image potential in the field.

Sometimes, though, that experience fails me.

Not long ago, as mentioned in the previous section, I discovered that Schenectady's Central Park had a rose garden. I went there armed with a Nikon D1 with an 18-55mm Nikon G lens mounted on it and a Nikon D70 with a Tamron D LD 70-300mm lens.

I knew walking up to the garden entrance I would get some good photos. It was a bright, sunny, clear day. Even though the Tamron was not the best lens — I'd only paid $29 for it — it still presented some interesting possibilities.

Even given that mindset, I was astonished at the number of beautiful, stunning flower photos I got that day. I shot 500 images between the two cameras.

So, I worked to process them all, separating the best, most stunning images out for a theme photo eBook.

Somewhere during the design and pagination of that eBook, I got the idea to try a few of the flower images as duotones.

Before we go on, I should explain what a duotone is.

You've seen them, but you may not know what they are called or how to apply the technique to your own photos.

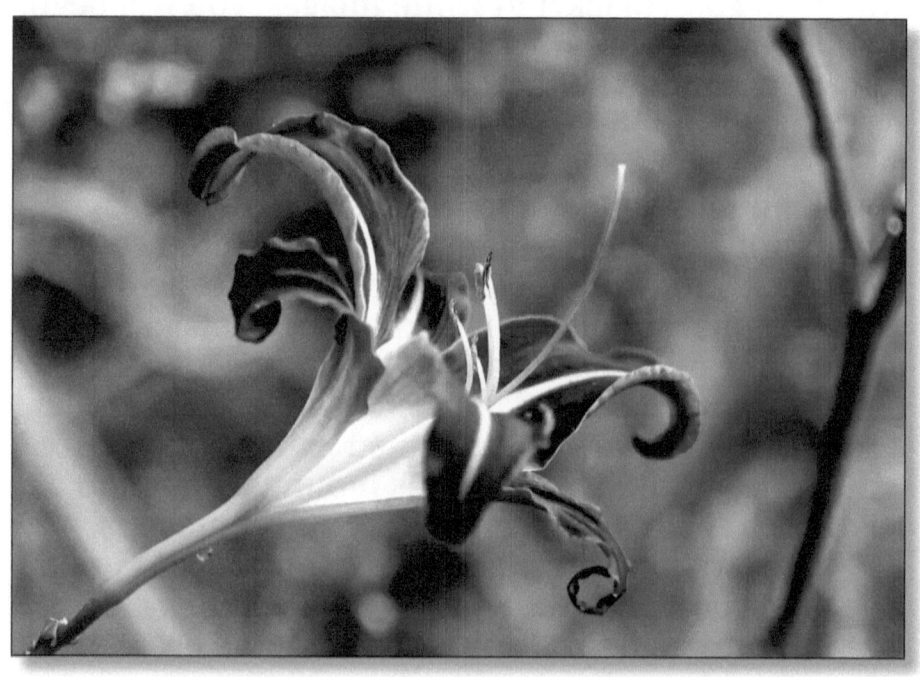

Central Park, Schenectady, NY, Aug. 17, 2014
Nikon D70, 165mm, 1/1000, f/4.8, ISO 400, Tv, pattern metering
Photo © 2014 by Shawn M. Tomlinson

Human beings are more inclined to like things they perceive as "warm" rather than "cold." A photo of a bright sunny scene with grass and trees in full bloom will draw the viewer in much more emotionally than the same scene with bright sun but covered in snow and ice.

It is a standard technique

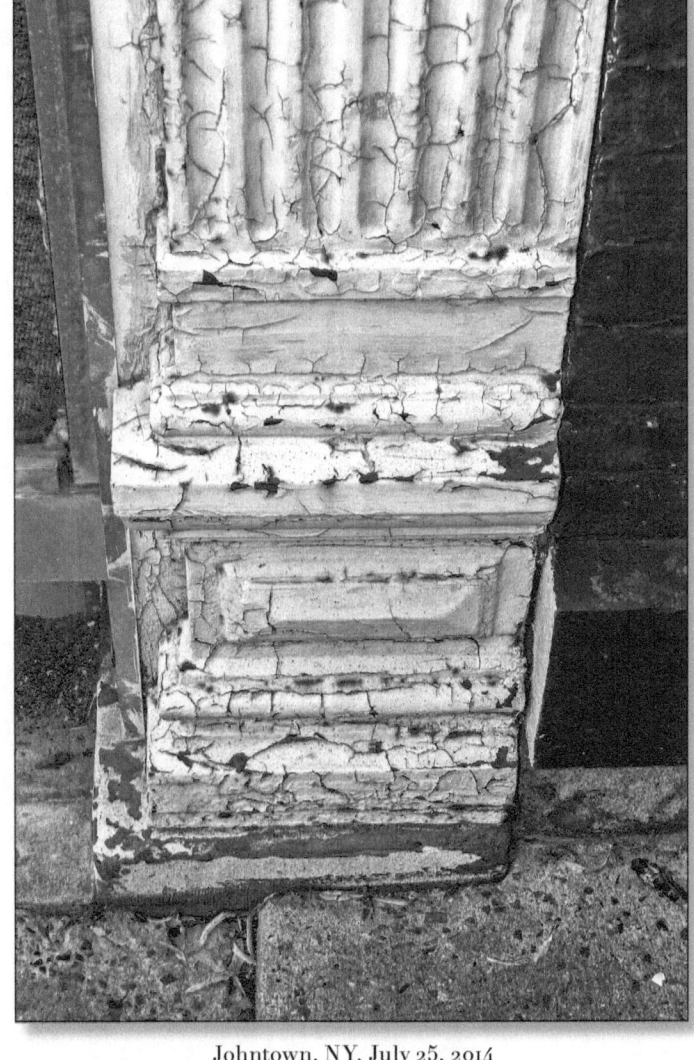

Johntown, NY, July 25, 2014
Pentax K20D, 40mm, 1/180, f/8, ISO 200, P, pattern metering
Photo © 2014 by Shawn M. Tomlinson

in print and other media to use warm colors — red, orange, pink, etc. — to produce a subconscious affinity for the subject in the viewer's mind. A certain fast food chain uses yellow and red in its signs, building colors and most of its products to produce a warm, comfortable, friendly feeling in customers and potential customers. This means they will think kindly about the "restaurant" no matter how horrible the "food" is.

When we still made photographs in the darkroom, there were two things we could do to utilize this effect. Photographic paper had basic tones in it before it was exposed and processed. The photographer could use warm or cold tone paper. Warm-tone paper had a slight brown or pink tint to it. Not enough so that you looked at a print and said, "That's brown or pink," but enough to subtly affect the mode of the image and the viewers. Cold-tone papers were more toward blue and gave a distant, unfriendly but often artistic appear-

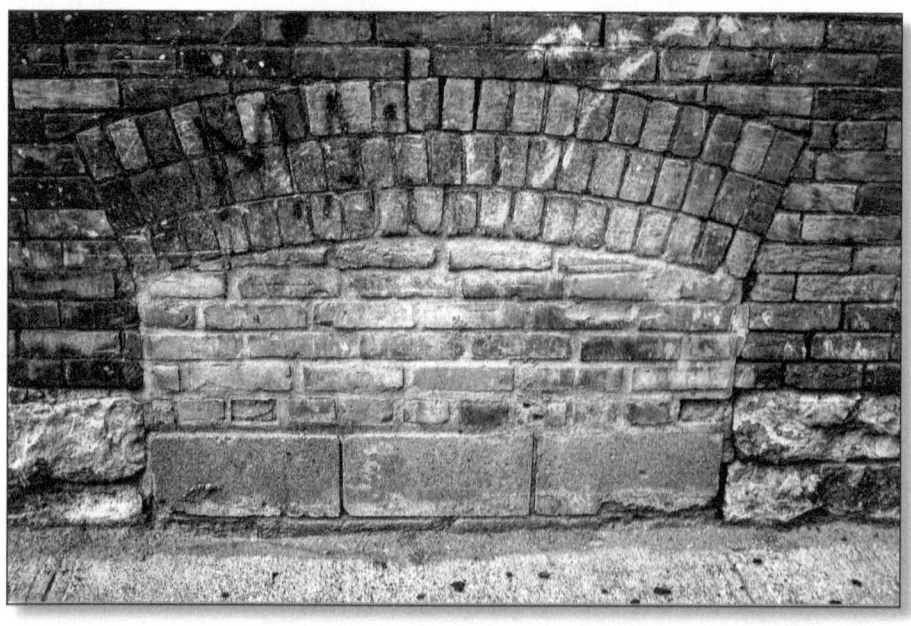

Saratoga Springs, NY, June 3, 2014
Canon EOS 20D, 28mm, 1/800, f/3.5, ISO 200, Tv, average metering
Photo © 2014 by Shawn M. Tomlinson

ance to images. Photographers also could use — and most did — neutral-tone photo paper for straight grayscale prints.

The other way we could affect tone was by using a toner. These came in various colors, but primarily brown, red and blue. If we used neutral-tone paper, developed the print, then immersed it in toner before using the fixer to stabilize the print, a color cast would be added.

Fortunately, this idea did not go away when photography turned digital. Adobe Photoshop has many presets to add toning to images. These include many simulations of historic toners such as sepia, selenium and gold. These are great, but they are obvious. If you use a sepia tone preset (Image>Adjustments>Gradient Map) it sets off in our minds that it is an old image. This is because we associate the brown-orange tint of sepia with images from the 19th century, particularly those of the American Civil War period. If that's what you want, great. There are lots of Gradient Map toning filters to accomplish it.

If, however, you want to give just a slight tone to your black and white images and keep them looking contemporary, there are two main ways to do it. For a detailed view of duotoning, see Part 5.

After that long-winded explanation, we're back where we started and what I did with those rose garden images. I started looking at the best flower photos and tried the duotone thing on them. I discovered it didn't work well on red or dark flowers, but on white an yellow, it could be amazing. Not with every image, but for those upon which this worked, well, they were stunning.

I know some people think that toning is cheating. Your photos now longer are grayscale if they have

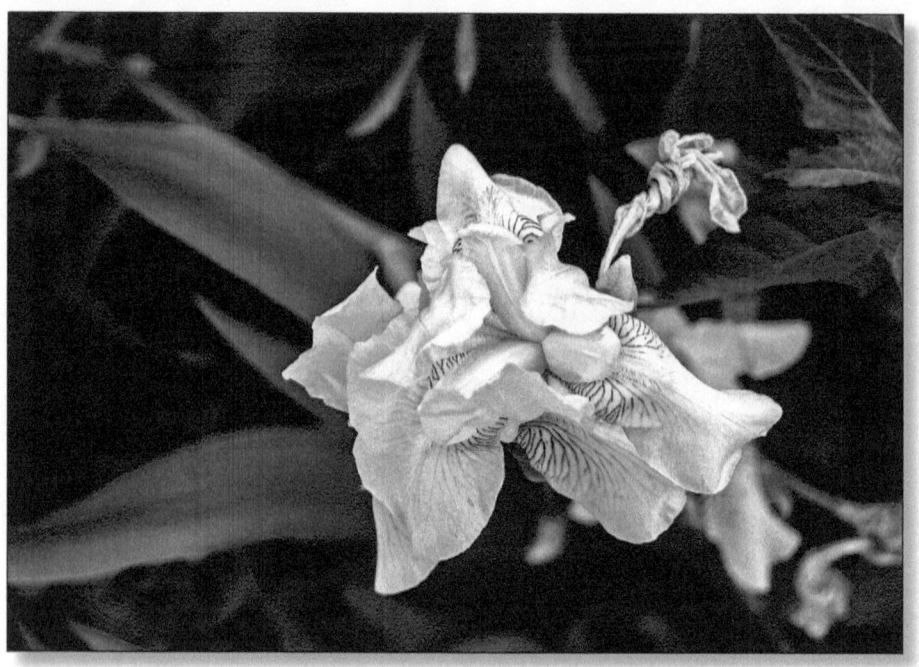

Saratoga Springs, NY, June 3, 2014
Canon EOS 20D, 80mm, 1/2500, f/5.6, ISO 200, Tv, average metering
Photo © 2014 by Shawn M. Tomlinson

even the slightest hint of color.

That's true, but who cares?

As far as I'm concerned, if Matthew Brady did it, then it has a 150-year precedent.

And — on some images — it looks fantastic.

If you start duotoning, you may go overboard with it, but soon you'll discover what types of images it enhances and what types it doesn't.

For example, it doesn't work too well on most photos with people in them. People in modern dress in modern surroundings tend to defeat the timelessness effect of duotones.

I use it sparingly. Many more photos look great in black and white than they do as duotones.

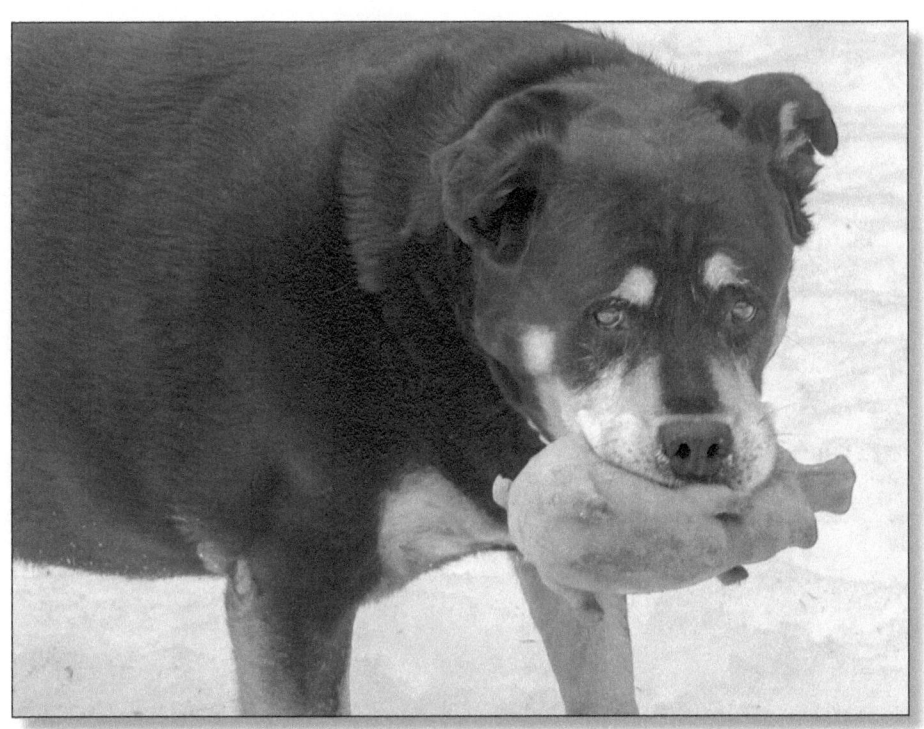

Ballston Lake, NY, March 25, 2015.
Nikon D2x, 130mm, 1/320, f/9, ISO 250, P, pattern metering
Photo © 2015 by Shawn M. Tomlinson

Most of the time I do not select subjects to photograph based upon what the images will look like as grayscale or duotone images. I may think they will look good in those forms, but I usually only make the decision later in Photoshop.

It is best to choose subjects that interest you, compose your images and shoot. You can always decide later if the photo is going to be your masterpiece "El Capitan" in Ansel Adams black and white. He didn't have that luxury, but you do.

Take advantage of it.

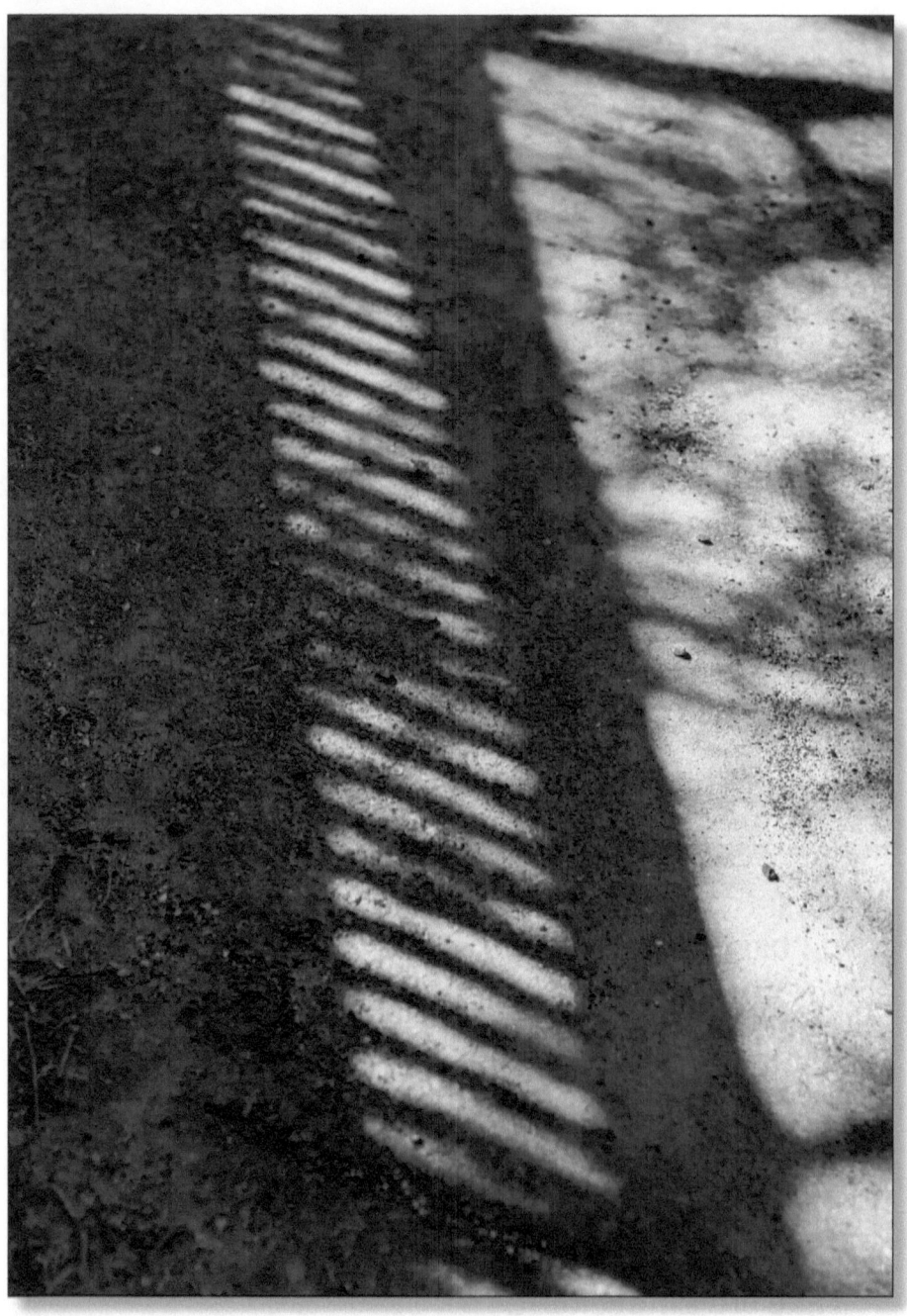

Saratoga Springs, NY, March 24, 2015.
Nikon D2x, 50mm, 1/1000, f/2.5, ISO 250, Tv, pattern metering
Photo © 2013, 2015 by Shawn M. Tomlinson

Ballston Lake, NY, April 2, 2015.
Nikon D2x, 10mm, 1/500, f/5.6, ISO 160, Tv, pattern metering
Photo © 2013, 2015 by Shawn M. Tomlinson

The Black & White Book • Page 57

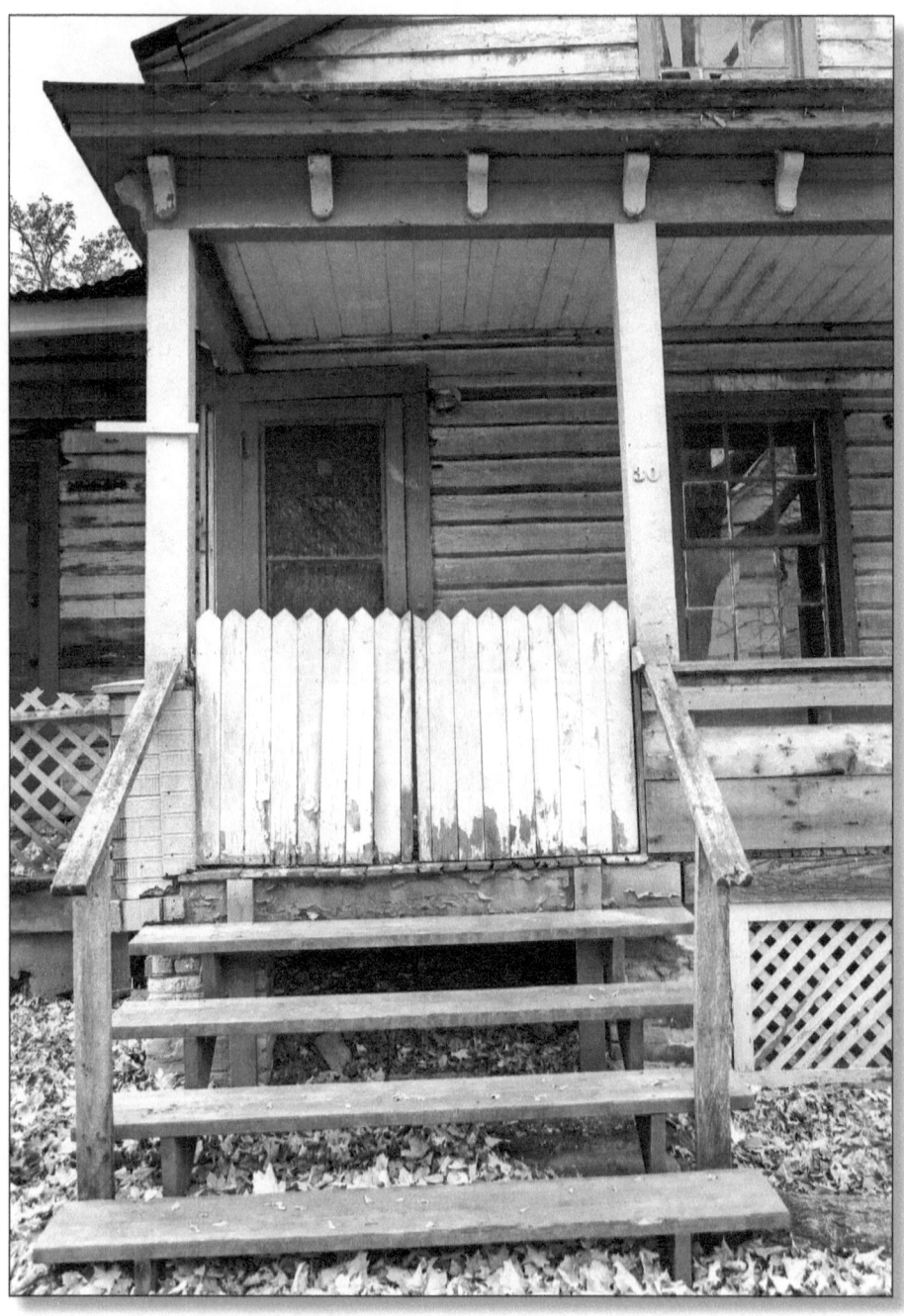

Saratoga Springs, NY, Nov. 1, 2014.
Nikon D7000, 18mm, 1/250, f/5, ISO 320, Tv, pattern metering
Photo © 2014, 2015 by Shawn M. Tomlinson

Part 5:

Doing the Ansel Adams Dance

People who saw Ansel Adams working in his darkroom described him as doing an elaborate dance, a ballet of pirouetting around the enlarger dodging here and burning there. He said himself that many of the resulting images the public saw were created largely in his darkroom.

Certainly he had a genius for seeing the composition in his head — he said, "A good photograph is knowing where to stand," he said — before setting up his large, 8-by-10-inch view camera, but once he captured the image, he had to spend hours or days with each one to get the prints he wanted.

Having stood in some of the same places Adams did in Yosemite Valley, I will admit that it is hard *not* to take a stunning photograph, even with a throwaway or iPhone camera. The place is just that photogenic. That said, though, millions of people have stood at Yosemite and no one ever has made photographs of it to the level Adams did.

Had he printed directly from his negatives without doing the dance, they still would have been good, but putting the effort into post-processing is what made his work legendary.

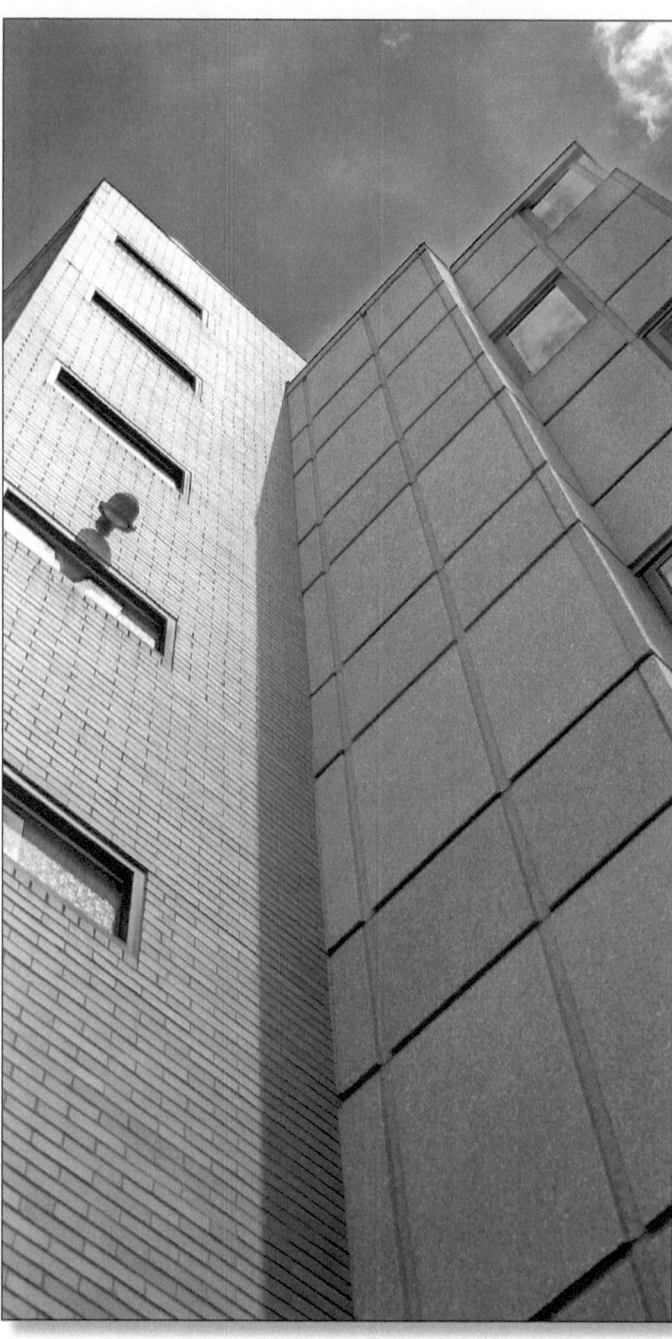

So, what's all this dodging and burning stuff?

With an enlarger it entails using two basic tools — with variations — to balance the print.

Dodging means that you lighten certain specific areas of the image, and burning means you darken sections.

The way Adams and every other photographer did this was to have homemade or

Saratoga Springs, NY, June 3, 2014
Canon EOS 20D, 28mm, 1/4000, f/3.5, ISO 200, Tv, averae metering
Photo © 2014 by Shawn M. Tomlinson

purchased tools.

The dodging tool was usually a flat round piece of cardboard on a stick of some sort. A thin stick or a stiff wire. As the negative was being expose to photo paper, the photographer would move this circular object around quickly in the areas he wanted lighter.

By blocking the light from the enlarger head even for a sec-

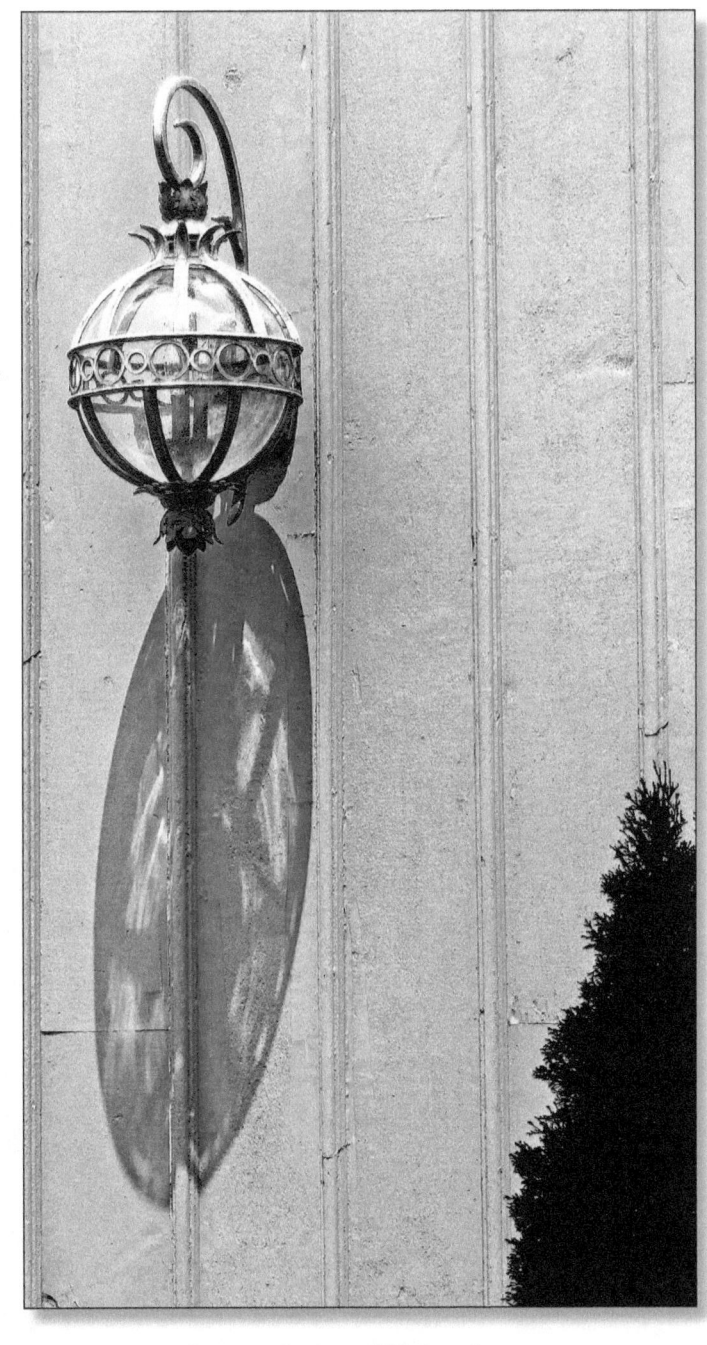

Saratoga Springs, NY, June 3, 2014
Canon EOS 20D, 60mm, 1/1000, f/7.1, ISO 200, Tv, average metering
Photo © 2014 by Shawn M. Tomlinson

ond or two, the area would be less exposed and lighter.

The burning tool was essentially the opposite of this: a piece of cardboard big enough to cover the entire projected area with a round hole cut in it.

By maneuvering this over the paper during enlarging, you could get more exposure to areas that needed it by "burning" them in.

Some photographers — including me — would just do this with their hands rather than the tools. This was especially useful if, for example, I needed to dodge two areas at once.

These were the main two tools Adams and others used during the enlargement process.

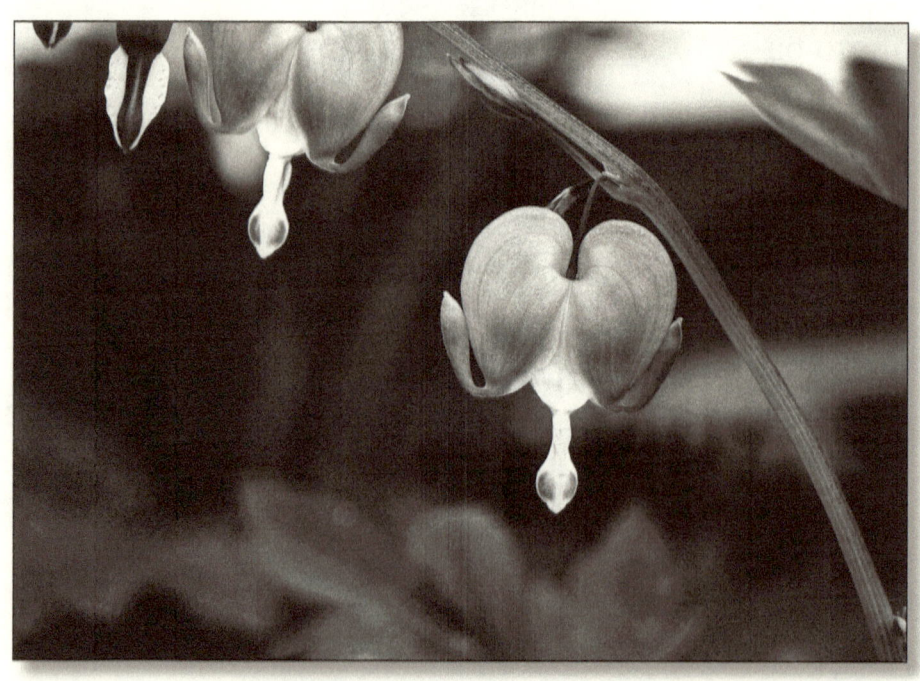

Ballston Lake, NY, June 1, 2014
Canon EOS 20D, 60mm, 1/320, f/5, ISO 400, Tv, average metering
Photo © 2014 by Shawn M. Tomlinson

Then there were the developing chemicals.

Often these were custom concoctions designed to bring out certain tones. The chemicals as well as time in them determined the final print.

Obviously, this is much easier now.

Photoshop has dodging and burning tools. The dodging tool looks like the aforementioned round thing on a stick, while the burning tool is in the shape of a hand. These tools work the same way as they did in the darkroom except that you don't have to work against the GraLab (timer) to get everything dodged and burned within the allotted exposure time.

Of course, the even better thing about using Photoshop and other photo-editing software is that you

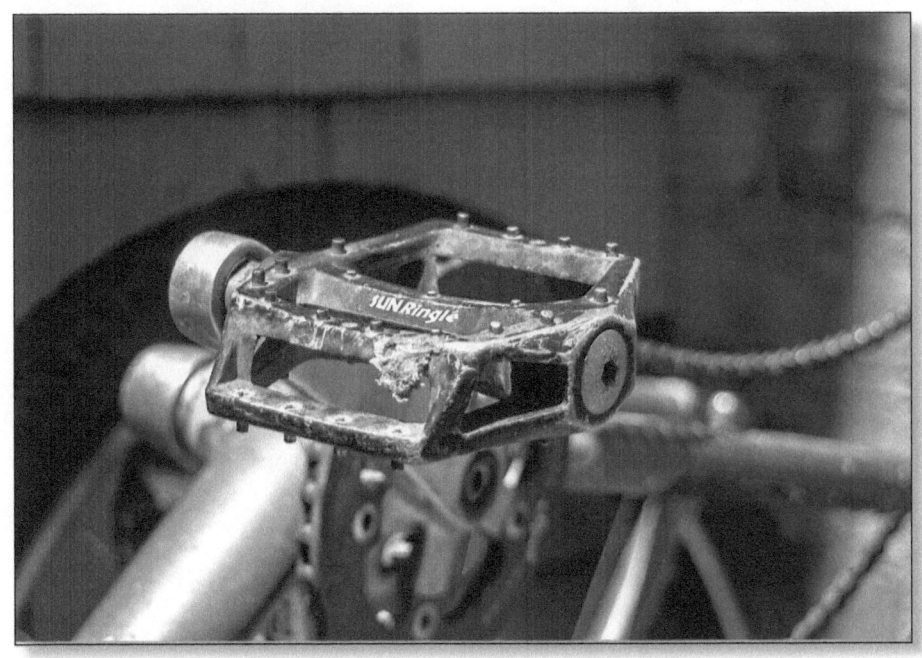

Saratoga Springs, NY, May 17, 2014
Nikon D1, 80mm, 1/320, f/5.6, ISO 200, Av, pattern metering
Photo © 2014 by Shawn M. Tomlinson

have a lot more tools available to you than Ansel ever did.

Too many, in fact. Some that you will be tempted to use and probably shouldn't, at least not very often.

OK, ya know what? *Do* use them.

Get it out of your system quickly so you can go back to making beautiful photo-graphs.

To make really good use of the tools in

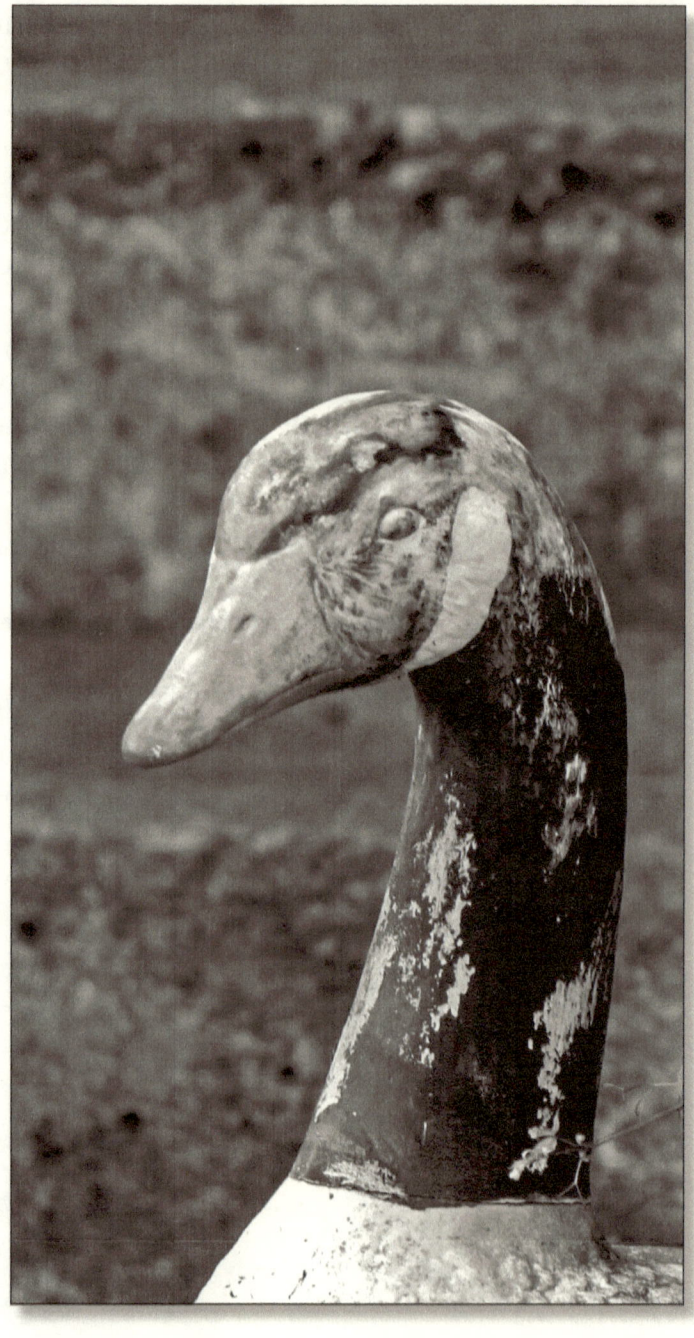

Ballston Lake, NY, July 29, 2014
Nikon D1, 300mm, 1/200, f/5.6, ISO 400, M, pattern metering
Photo © 2014 by Shawn M. Tomlinson

Photoshop to create those beautiful black and white photos, here are some guidelines. There is a different process for duotones.

This is just what I do and as you experiment and learn you may find better ways of doing things.

First, before you get started, **DO NOT USE** the Grayscale selection under Image>Mode.

Using this severely limits your control of and adjustments to your images. It removes enormous amounts of data that you need to make the best black and white images you can.

Likewise, **DO NOT USE** the Desaturate selection under Image>Adjustments. This is better than switching the Mode from RGB to Grayscale, but not

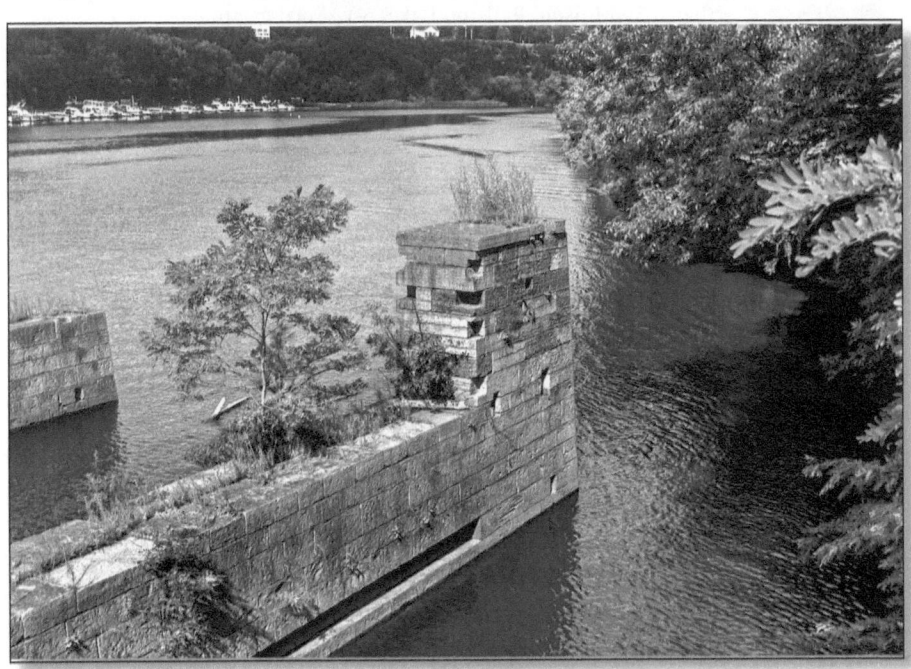

Aqueduct, Rexford, NY, July 16, 2014
Nikon D1, 28mm, 1/1250, f/3.5, ISO 200, Av, pattern metering
Photo © 2014 by Shawn M. Tomlinson

much.

The way the pros used to make black and white conversions in Photoshop for optimum image quality was to go to Image>Adjustments, click the Monochrome checkbox and adjust the Red, Green and Blue sliders.

Adobe's people constantly got feedback that this was the best way to make subtle adjustments and the best black and white images, so the designers created the Black & White control panel under Image>Adjustments.

This gives even better and more subtle control over image tone and quality.

So:

1) Make your adjustments in the Camera RAW Workspace as you normally would for a color photo, then open it in Photoshop.

2) Save your image as the RGB version in TIFF format.

3) Save it again (File>Save As) still in the RGB and TIFF formats, with a different name.

A) If you are going to make many B&W images, you may want to create a special designation for them in the file names.

B) I have a very specific system for naming photo files and if you handle a lot of them — You're a *pho-*

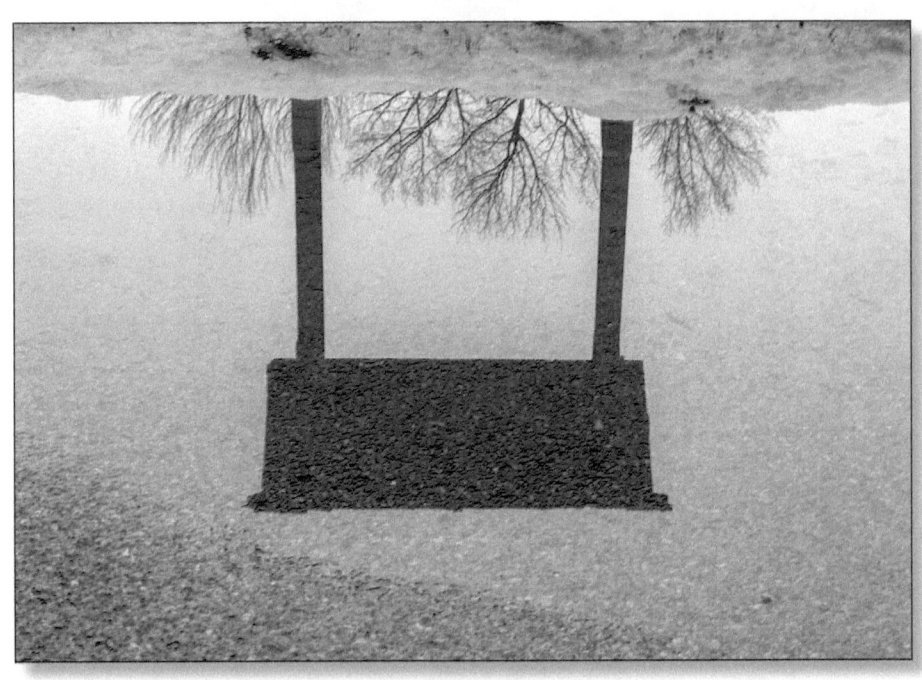

Boat Launch, Broadalbin, NY, April 4, 2014
Canon EOS 10D, 42mm, 1/15, f/16, ISO 200, P, pattern metering
Photo © 2014 by Shawn M. Tomlinson

tographer. You will — create your own. As an example, a typical photo file of mine has a name such as:

2014 1208 A RX D7k 001 DSC_9671. tif

What it means:
2014 = year
1208 = date (Dec. 8)
A = which pho-to session that day; A, B, C, etc.
RX = location (Rexford)
D7k = cam-era used (Nikon

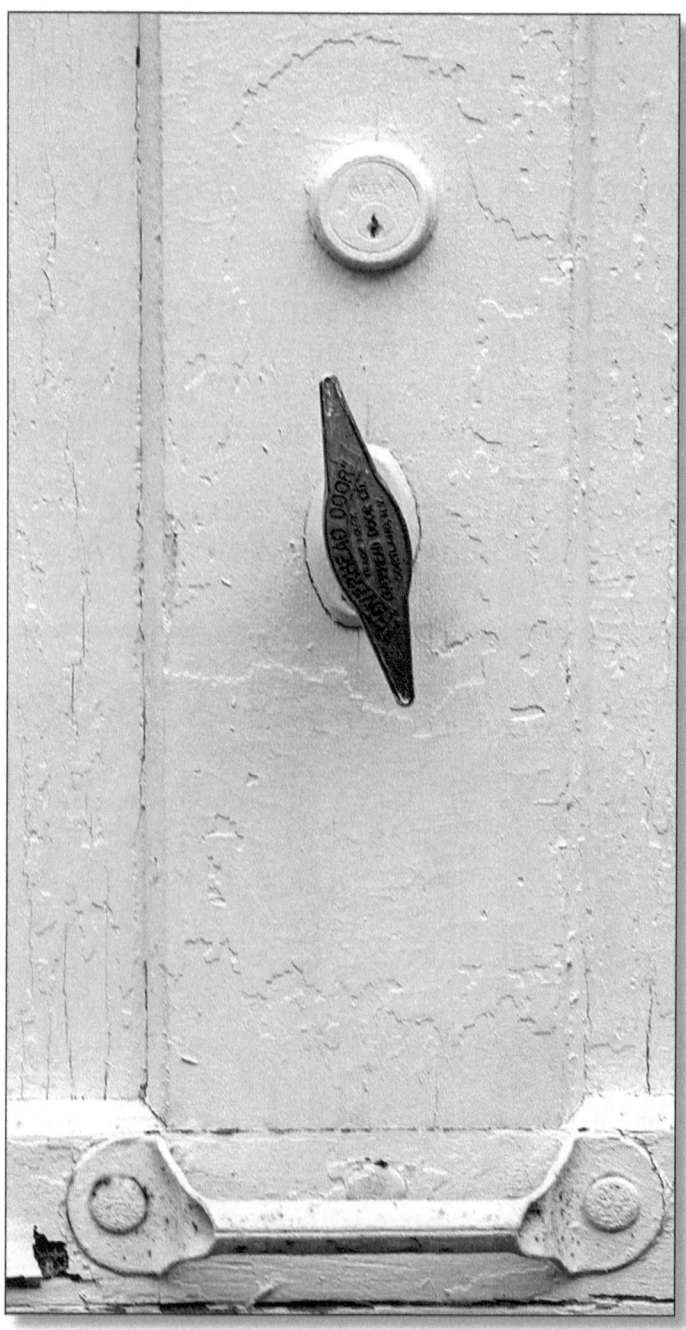

Saratoga Springs, NY, April 5, 2014
Canon EOS 10D, 80mm, 1/250, f/10, ISO 200, P, pattern metering
Photo © 2014 by Shawn M. Tomlinson

D7000)

001 = number of photo in sequence (this is the first photo in the "A" sequence)

DSC_ 9671 = camera's file code (created by the camera during shooting; I keep this number as part of the file name because it makes it easier to find the original RAW file when I need it)

.tif = file type assigned by Photoshop when you save and

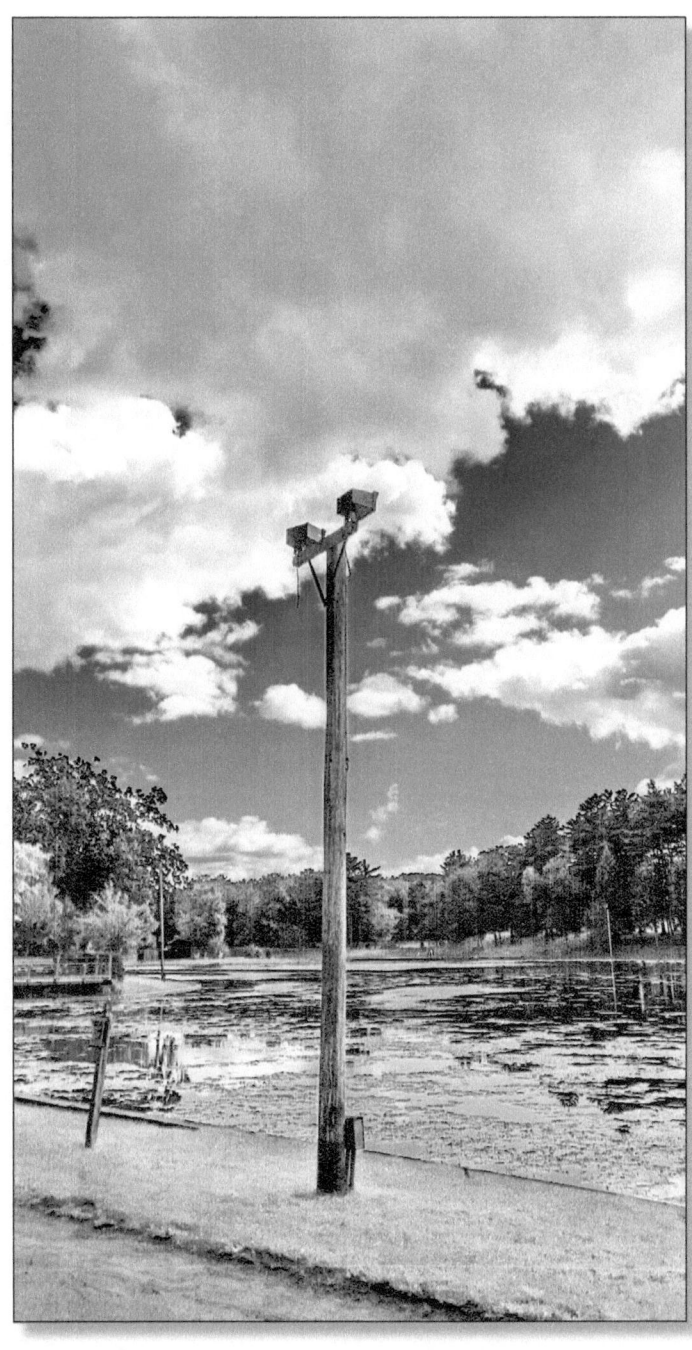

Central Park, Schenectady, Aug. 17, 2014
Nikon D1, 18mm, 1/1600, f/5.6, ISO 200, Av, pattern metering
Photo © 2014 by Shawn M. Tomlinson

select TIFF

So, when I am saving a copy of the same photo as a B&W image, I add a "G" (Grayscale; shorter than B&W if not wholly accurate) in the name:

2014 1208 A RX D7k 001 DSC_9671 G.tif

For a toned version of the same photo, the file name would be:

2014 1208 A RX D7k 001 DSC_9671 T.tif

4) Go to Image>Adjustments>Black & White. The

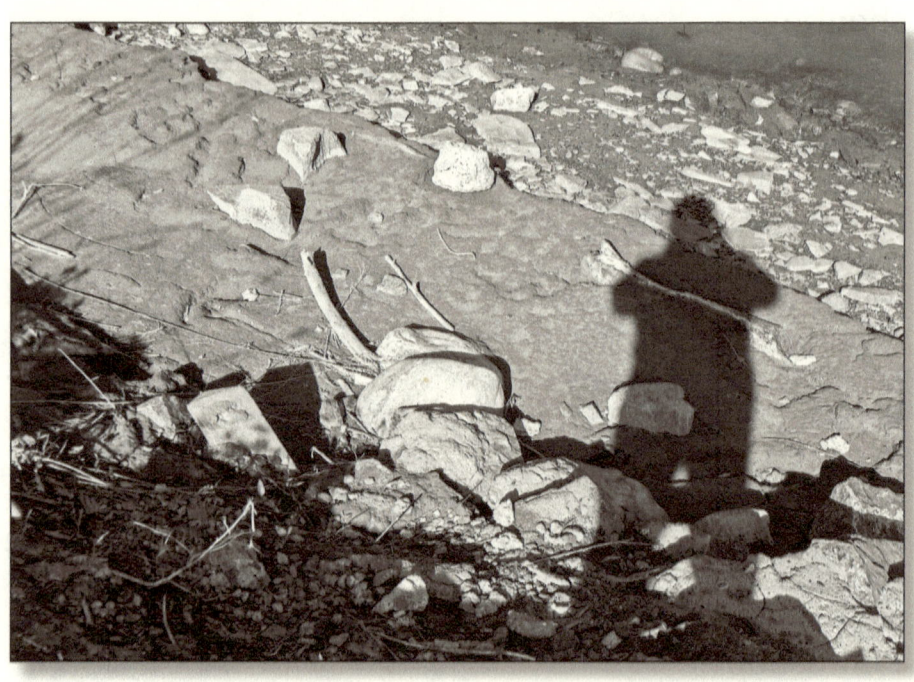

Freeman's Bridge, NY, May 12, 2014
Canon EOS 10D, 37mm, 1/200, f/8, ISO 200, P, pattern metering
Photo © 2014 by Shawn M. Tomlinson

moment you do this, the image will change on your screen to black and white, but don't stop there.

5) Use the color sliders — Reds, Yellows, Greens, Cyans, Blues and Magentas — to make your adjustments while you watch the preview image.

A) You may wonder why.

This is crazy, you think.

The photo is *grayscale*; it doesn't *have* reds, yellows, greens, etc., in it.

It does, though.

By using your photo with in RGB (red-green-blue), format, the standard color space used in Photoshop and elsewhere, still intact, you have access to this digital information, which you would not have if you switched to Grayscale.

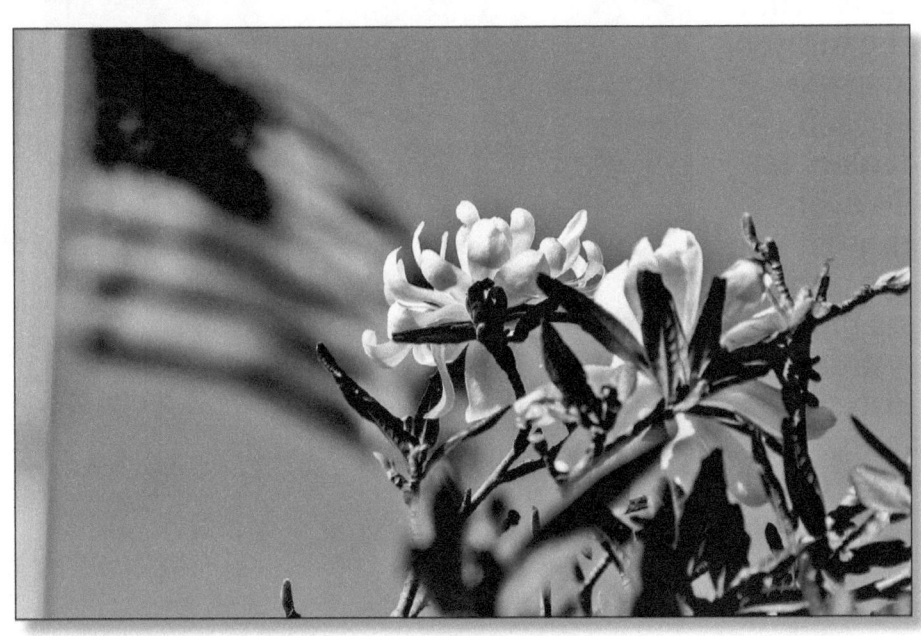

Freeman's Bridge, NY, May 12, 2014
Canon EOS 10D, 200mm, 1/400, f/8, ISO 200, P, pattern metering
Photo © 2014 by Shawn M. Tomlinson

RGB has millions of levels of color and grayscale only has those 256 shades of gray. Photoshop doesn't care if the image *appears* RGB or grayscale to humans; it only cares what the numeric value of each "color" is. So even though you are only *seeing* a 256-level grayscale image on your display, Photoshop still "sees" it as a millions-level

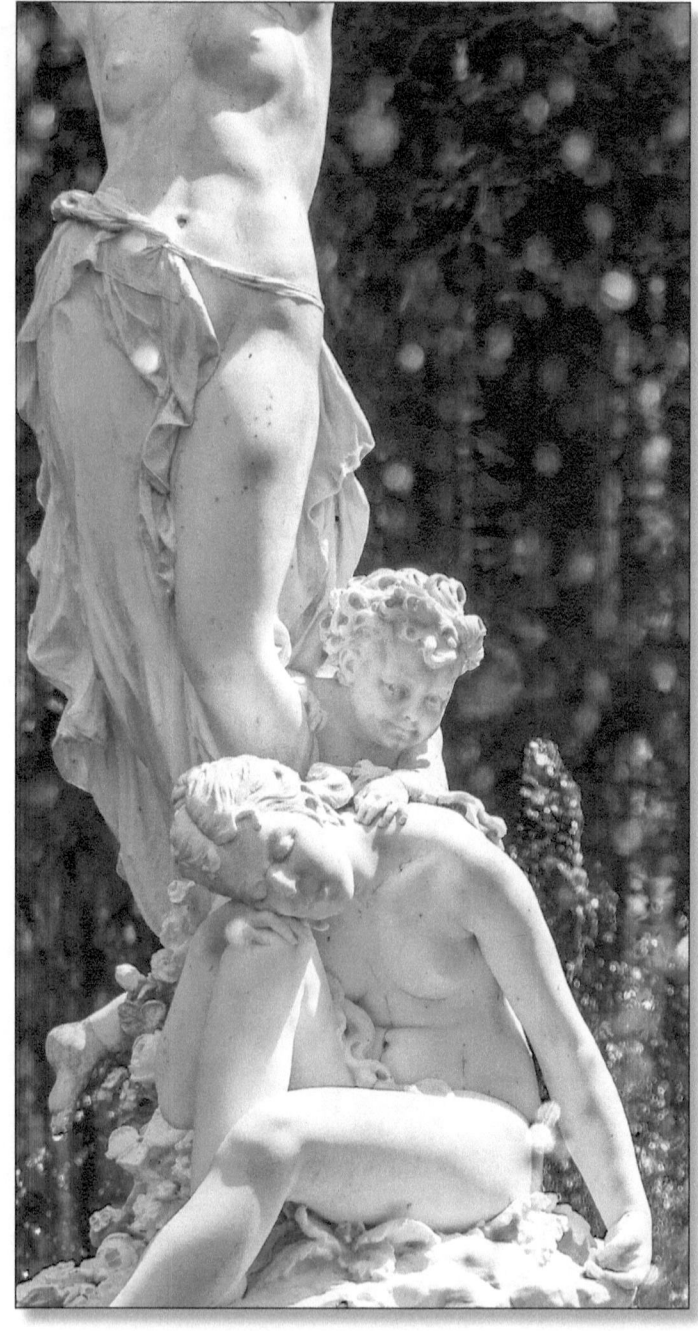

Yaddo, Saratoga Springs, NY, May 10, 2014
Pentax K20D, 200mm, 1/350, f/8, ISO 100, P, pattern metering
Photo © 2014 by Shawn M. Tomlinson

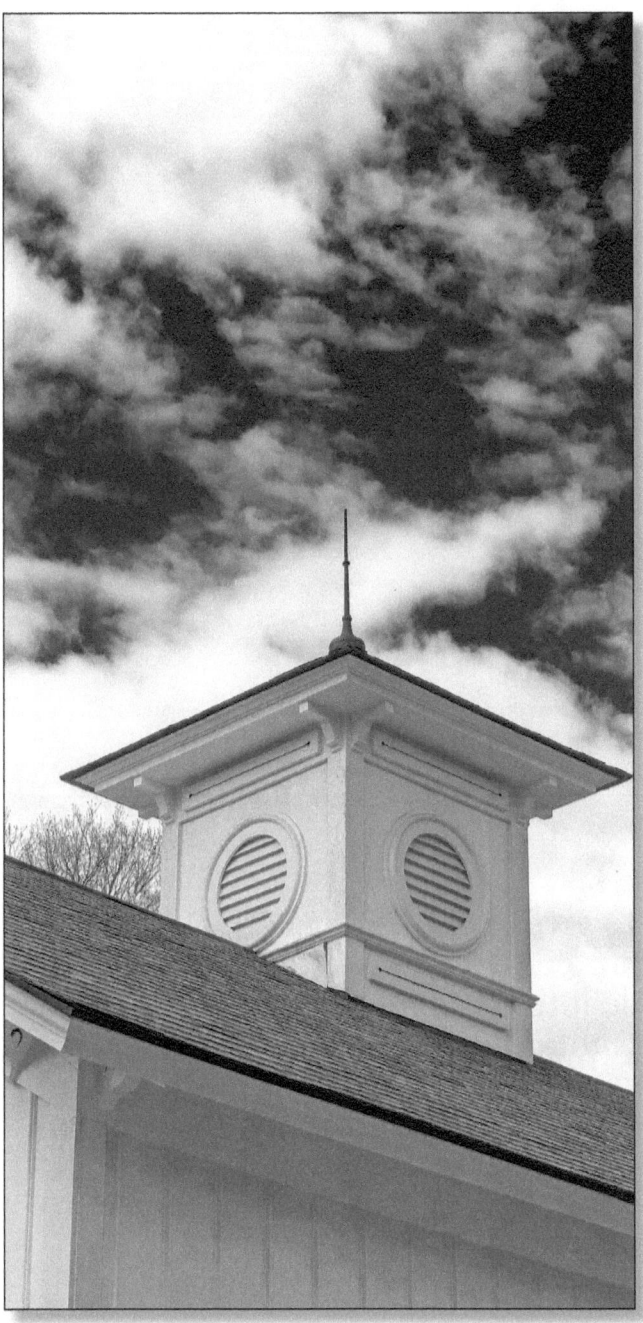

Saratoga Springs, NY, May 2, 2015.
Nikon D2x, 50mm, 1/800, f/9, ISO 400, Tv, pattern metering
Photo © 2015 by Shawn M. Tomlinson

RGB.

I know this is confusing, so let's try it in practical terms.

You've just shot a fantastic autumn scene in which one tree's leaves are astonishingly yellow. The color just leaps off your display.

Oooo. Wouldn't that look good in grayscale?

So, you go to Image>Adjustments>Black & White.

Suddenly, the image is all flat gray. The yellow has virtually merged with everything else and nothing looks

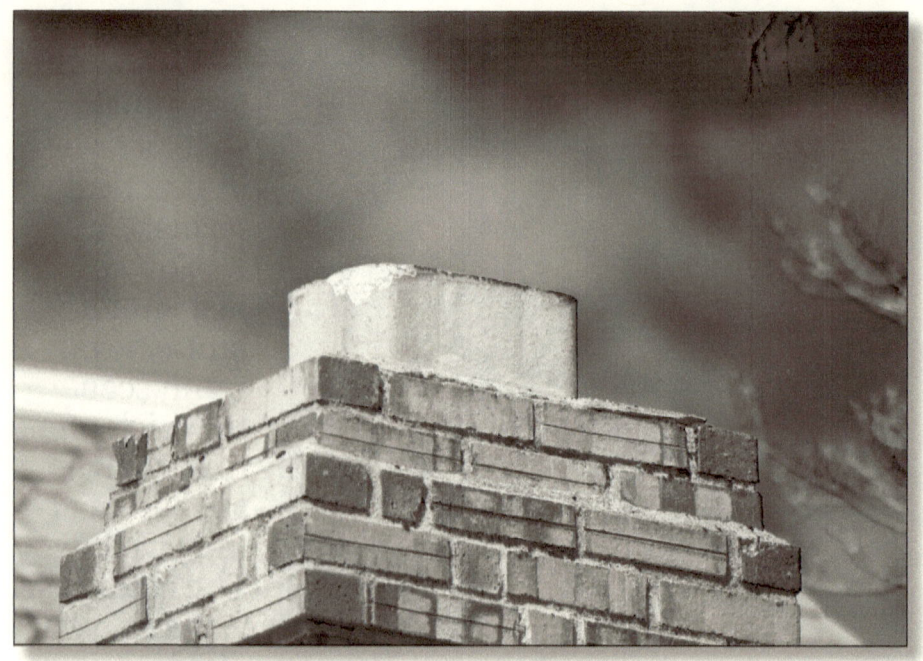

Saratoga Springs, NY, April 18, 2015.
Nikon D2x, 300mm, 1/1000, f/5.6, ISO 400, Tv, pattern metering
Photo © 2015 by Shawn M. Tomlinson

good.

You're about to give up when you look at those sliders. One is marked "Yellow" so, you figure, what the hell? You slide it to the right and — Oh My! — the leaves become bright. Slide the "Red" to the right a bit, and it gets even better. Slide "Cyan" and "Blue" a touch to the left — darkening the sky a bit — and now you have a good black and white image.

You didn't see the yellows as yellows in the monochrome image, but Photoshop did.

That's why this is the best method for creating stellar B&W images.

6) Click the OK button to get back to Photoshop's

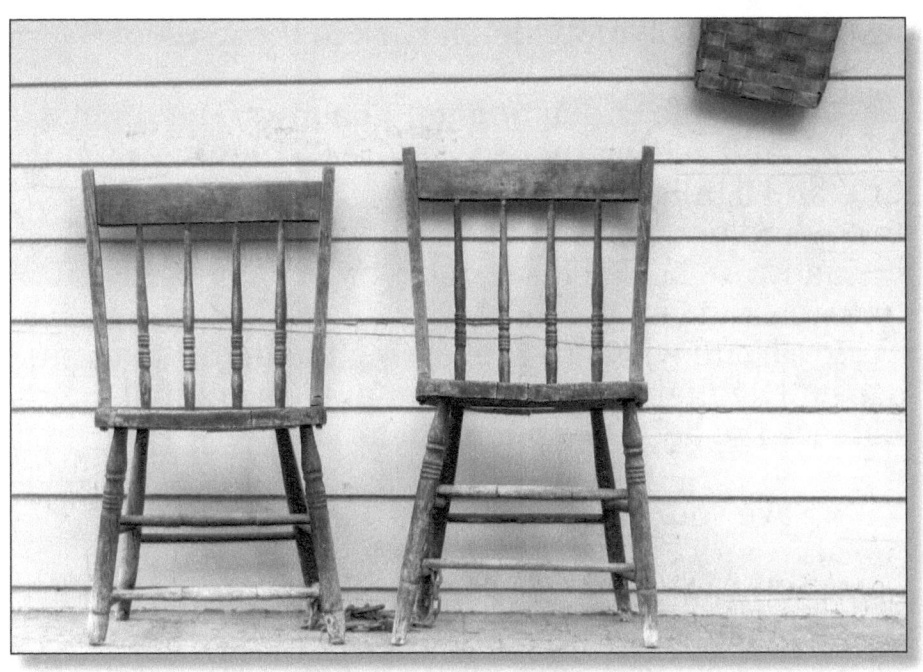

Saratoga Springs, NY, May 2, 2015.
Nikon D2x, 50mm, 1/1600, f/2.2, ISO 400, Tv, pattern metering
Photo © 2015 by Shawn M. Tomlinson

main pane.

7) Go to Image>Adjustments>Levels, if the image already is not perfectly to your liking. You can use the sliders of Levels to tone down the brights, bring up the blacks, give more details in the midtones.

8) Use Shadows/Highlights.
A) If you lost some detail in the bright areas, another way to recapture those details is to use Shadows/Highlights.
Most people use this only to lighten shadows, but it has other uses, too.
In this case, assuming your shadows are fine, you

just want a little more detail back in those yellow-now-white leaves.

Go to Image>Adjustments>Shadows/Highlights. The default setting that appears is Shadows: Amount: 35% an Highlights: Amount: 0%. Change Shadows to 0% and use the Highlights slider to regain detail. I usually use between 8% and 15%, but choose what looks best to you.

Be careful with this tool. Using too high a percentage on Highlights can create an unpleasant, flat effect. Balance the detail with the brightness.

9) Save your photo as an RGB in the TIFF file format.

A) Why in RGB?

You could, once you are finished with all your adjustments, convert your image to Grayscale Mode. It would be a smaller file and take up less room on your hard drive.

Don't.

If you plan to print your image or publish it in electronic format — Kindle, iPad, etc. — RGB files just work better. I'm not even certain why exactly, but they do.

B) Why in TIFF?

As stated, JPEG is a compressed file format. Each file takes less hard drive space than a TIFF or other format file. To compress the file, JPEG throws out data that is necessary for your image to appear and print as you intended. The format also tends to increase RGB noise and artifacts that decrease the image quality.

You're a *photographer*.

Save **ALL** your images as RGB and TIFF.

The one exception is if you need to print your pho-

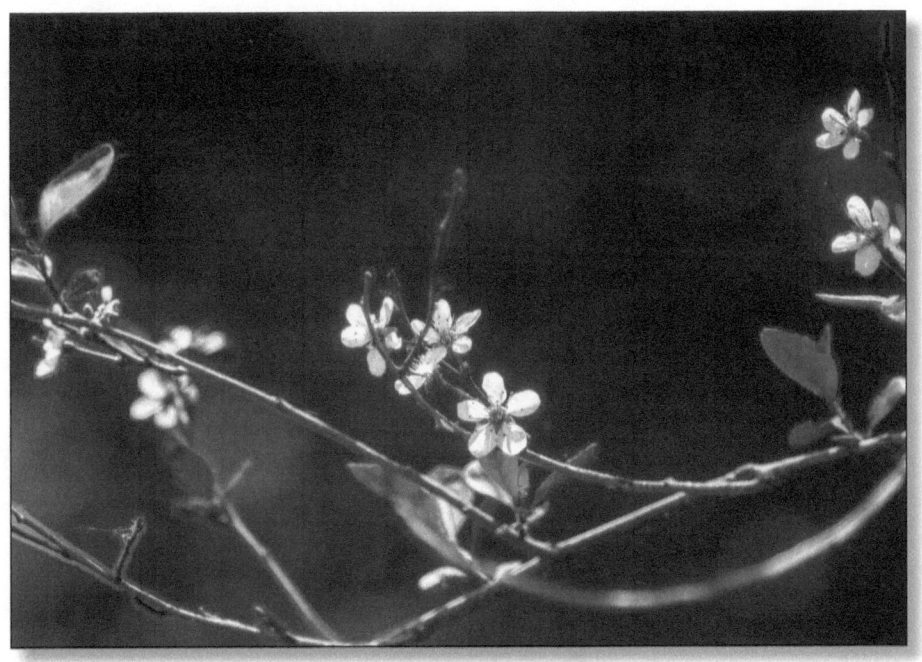

Ballston Lake, NY, May 10, 2015.
Nikon D2x, 300mm, 1/640, f/5.6, ISO 400, Tv, pattern metering
Photo © 2015 by Shawn M. Tomlinson

to in a newspaper or magazine that requires special formatting.

In these cases, go with what the printer requires, usually CMYK in TIFF, PDF, DCS 1 or DCS 2 formats.

A note here about grain.

One of the things we photographers loved and hated about black and white film was grain.

The beloved and lamented Kodak Tri-X Pan film produced a particularly grainy image because it had a high ASA speed rating. ASA became ISO, and it got translated into light sensitivity with digital cameras. Tri-X Pan was 400 ASA/ISO. Now, 400 ISO on a DSLR produces almost no grain.

The higher you push the ISO on your DSLR, the grainier the images get. Camera manufacturers have worked very hard to eliminate grain and the digital equivalent, noise, especially in top-end cameras such as the Canon EOS 1Dx and the Nikon D4s.

The thing is, though, that especially in black and white images, grain is not a bad thing. It can add texture to images and even give a hint of nostalgia.

Adobe Photoshop lets you add film grain to your images, but it doesn't really look realistic.

I've found that, if you want grain, probably the best way to get it is to increase the ISO sensitivity on your DSLR. How much will depend on the camera, but generally up around 800 to 6400.

Although I do not do this on purpose, I have found that when I need to push up the ISO to 800, especially on my Nikon D2x, I get a good amount of color noise. I can eliminate the RGB artifacts usually with Photoshop, but I don't need to if I'm making a B&W photo. Once I convert it, the noise turns to grain and gives a good effect.

To more effectively emulate specific types of film grain, such as Tri-X Pan, there actually are programs with film emulation filters available.

Part 6:

Duotoning

Duotones are popular, perhaps too popular, but with the right images, they really work.

I know I covered this to some extent earlier, but duotoning really deserves its own section.

Duotoning, essentially, is a modern version of toning photographs. I mentioned earlier that sepia was one of the first tones used, more to give stability to the prints than to render them brown and whites. If you are not sure what a sepia-toned print is, take a look at Ken Burn's documentary, *The Civil War*, or any photographs from that era.

Although probably not originally intended, the sepia made the images give a "warmer" impression of the image to the views. This worked especially well on portraits where long exposures usually required the subjects to sit or stand in the exact same position for many minutes. Their expressions often looked pained, but the warmer brownish tone of sepia helped soften this.

Of course, nothing including sepia could make American Civil War images warmer. But sepia did preserve them so we can see them now.

Once true black and white was possible and stable, some photographers realized that it could give a cold or severe look to images. Sometimes this works, but generally not for people.

This led back to the use of toners to change black and white images, and then led to the creation of differently toned photo paper.

When I was working in the darkroom, I discovered warmer and colder tone papers and used them to different effect. They were less messy and worked better for me than toners. Red toner, for example, was supposed to give a slightly warm tone to images, but I usually got pink.

Warm-toned photo paper usually gave a slight hint of the warmer brown without being overwhelming.

Again, it didn't work for everything.

Naturally, all this carried over into digital photography.

Photoshop and other digital photo editing software make it easy to add tones or change colors around.

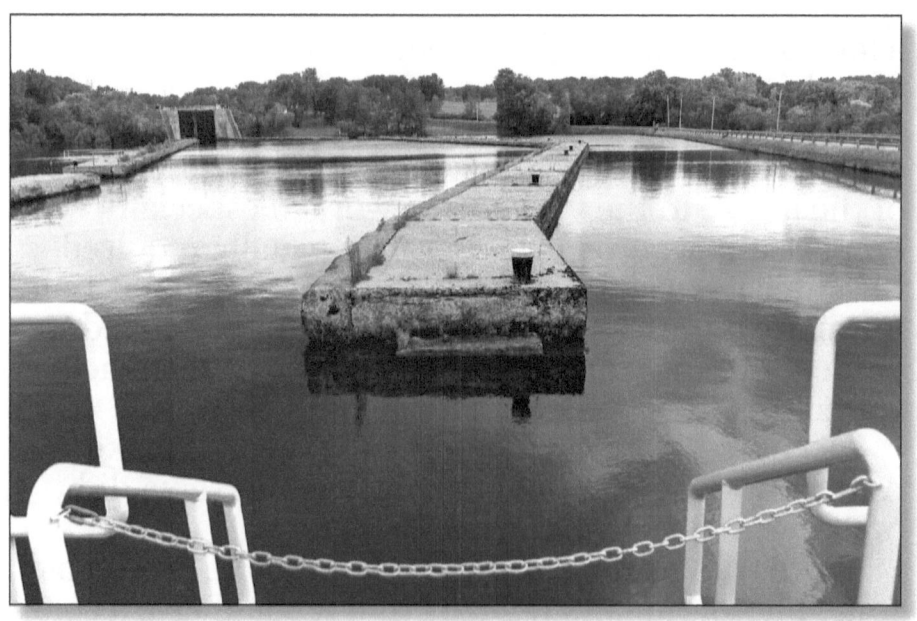

Waterford, NY, Sept. 6, 2014
Canon EOS 1Ds, 30mm, 1/160, f/8, ISO 250, P, pattern metering
Photo © 2014 by Shawn M. Tomlinson

Using the right colors to tone can produce some spectacular images.

I should point out here, as I have elsewhere in this book, that in the original version of this book, it was possible to reproduce the duotoned images accurately because it was available only as an eBook. It costs no more, nor is it any more difficult to produce duotoned or color images in an eBook that it does to produce B&W images.

Unfortunately, in this new expanded print version, only B&W images are possible.

To see some examples of duotoned images from this book, look at the front and back covers, and go to the eBook version at:

http://www.amazon.com/gp/product/B00QW-5P9UI?*Version*=1&*entries*=0

So, to make duotones of your images, you can use one of two methods in Adobe Photoshop. It used to be simpler than this, but those at Adobe decided to remove the Variations tool. About two clicks used to do it, but now it's a little more complicated. On the bright side, the resulting images do look better, at least to me.

Start with your RAW image, open it to the Camera RAW Workspace and make the adjustments you normally would for a color image. Then open the image in the main Photoshop interface and make any further adjustments you choose. Save the file as a color TIFF image, then save it a second time, also as a TIFF, but label it something else. I usually add a "T" at the end of the file name.

This will be the file you will turn into a duotone.

The simpler of the two methods for duotoning at

this point is to go to Image>Adjustments>Black and White.

Down at the bottom is a checkbox next to the word Tint. Beneath that are two slider controls, Hue and Saturation. Clicking the checkbox sets Hue to 42° and Saturation to 20 percent. Change Saturation to 6 to 8 percent and you will get a slight warm tone to your image quite like sepia toning.

You can do it this way and it generally looks OK. I did this for some early toning attempts, but it never gave me exactly the type of tone I wanted.

Someone pointed out to me as though I should have known it all along that Photoshop provides specific tools for duotones.

It even has many preset options.

As with just about everything in Photoshop, I may select a preset, but then tweak it to my liking. I rarely stay with any preset as it is.

Which leads to the second method, which is a little more complicated, but produces a wonderful effect. To make these duotones of your images, you need to follow a different and somewhat counter-intuitive path.

Before you start, though, it works best to go to Adjustments>Black and White and make the best use of the sliders to produce the best image to your eye.

The photo still will be in RGB (red-green-blue) Mode at this point, and duotoning with this method doesn't work in RGB.

So, go to Image>Mode>Grayscale.

Yes, I know I said never to make a black and white image using Grayscale Mode, but you already have made the best black and white image you can in RGB.

Changing it at this point to Grayscale Mode will not show a perceptible change.

Once your image is in grayscale, go back to Image>Mode and select Duotone.

Photoshop provides many preset combinations to produce a variety of Duotone effects.

The one I use most consists of Black and Pantone Warm Gray 8 CVC.

I set that, click OK, then go to the Levels adjustment to tweak the blacks, whites and midtones to get exactly the duotone I want.

If you use this method, after you get to the precise adjustments you want, remember to go back to Image>Mode and select RGB. This is very important because if you leave it in duotone mode, you can't save the file to TIFF, but only PSD, Photoshop's native file format.

Here is a step-by-step checklist to make duotones this way.

1) So, OK, as with the above, make your initial adjustments in the Camera RAW Workspace.

2) Open the image in Photoshop and make any further adjustments you need.

3) Save the color image as a TIFF in RGB Mode.

4) Save it again with a different file name.

5) Go to Image>Mode>Grayscale. Yes, I know I said not to use Grayscale Mode, but in this case it works, so hang on.

6) Go to Image>Mode>Duotone. At the top of the Duotone dialog box you will see a scroll bar with "Preset:" next to it. You can click the scroll bar to select a preset while looking at your image to get the tone you want. The one I use shows Black in the top box and PANTONE Warm Gray 8 CVC in the second box. The word "Duotone" should be selected next to the "Type:" setting.

7) Click OK and it returns to the main Photoshop pane.

8) Go to Image>Adjustments>Levels and tweak the sliders under the histogram to get the exact tone you like. I usually increase both the Blacks (left slider) and the Whites (right slider) a bit each, depending upon the dynamics of the image.

9) Go to Image>Mode>RGB.

10) Save your image.

Part 7:

Printing

Printing, as I said, can be quite tricky for black and white photographs.

Most ink jet printers are designed for color photographs, so their inks and software are calibrated for color.

Because all full-color images have black in them, common ink jet printers have one or more black inks, but for some reason the printer manufacturers do not allow you to turn off the color inks. It seems like this would be easy enough to program into the printers, but none that I have found do it.

So, when you tell your printer to print grayscale images, the printer's software tells it to combine various percentages of all the ink cartridges to make the shades of gray from black to white. Even on good, relatively expensive larger format printers, this process can create an unwanted color tint to your black and white images.

To reiterate, there are several things you can do to get really good black and white images printed.

1) Go to a professional printer. Not department stores or drugstores, but real printers. If you do not have one near you, there are many online services available. You upload your image file, pay, they print it and mail you your prints. This is especially important — using professional labs nearby or online — if

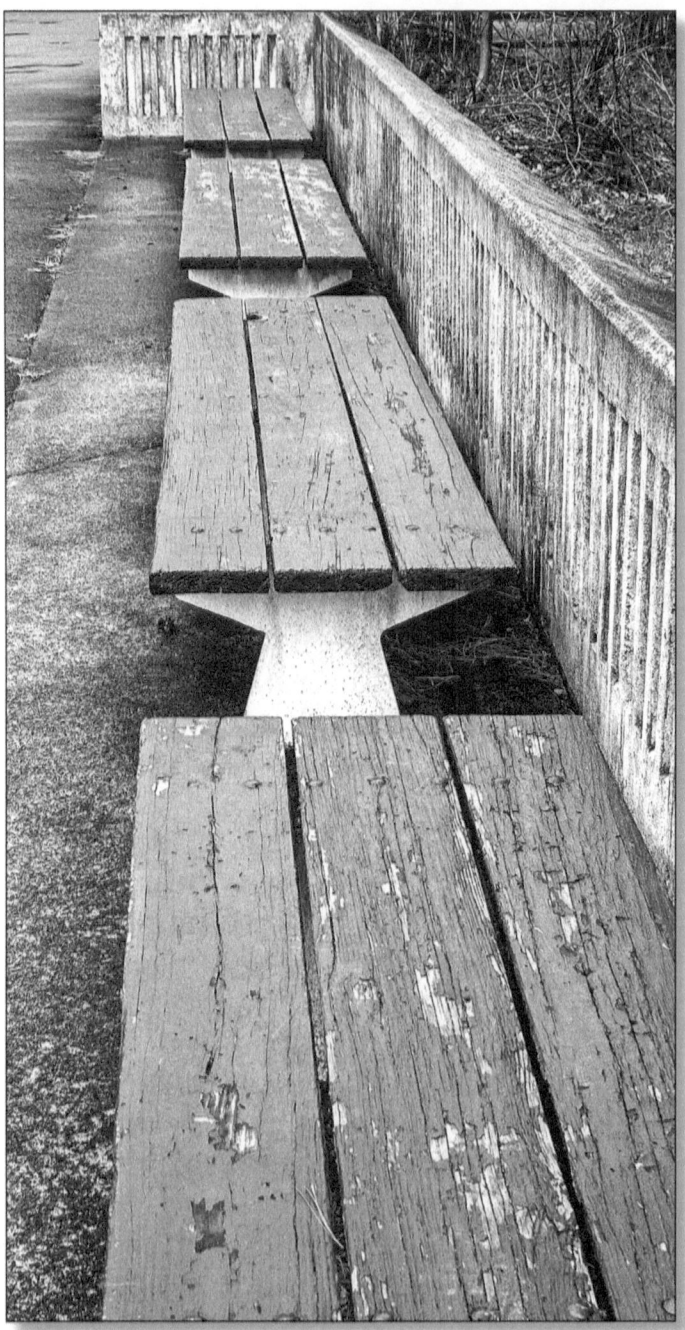

your photos are going to be exhibited. You don't want a sickly green or magenta color cast destroying all the work you put into creating your images, and you don't want potential reviewers and buyers to get a subconscious "yech" feeling from your images.

2) Get a black and white printer. These are not cheap and there aren't that many available,

Saratoga Performing Arts Center, Saratoga Springs, NY, May 3, 2014
Canon EOS 20D, 28mm, 1/500, f/8, ISO 400, P, pattern metering
Photo © 2014 by Shawn M. Tomlinson

but they are the second best thing to having your black and white images printed by a lab. Not only are the printers themselves expensive, but the inks — of which there may be many — are quite expensive, too. Good photo paper also is not cheap.

Let's consider a typical set up and the current costs.

Epson Stylus Pro 3880 = $1,295 retail

Nine

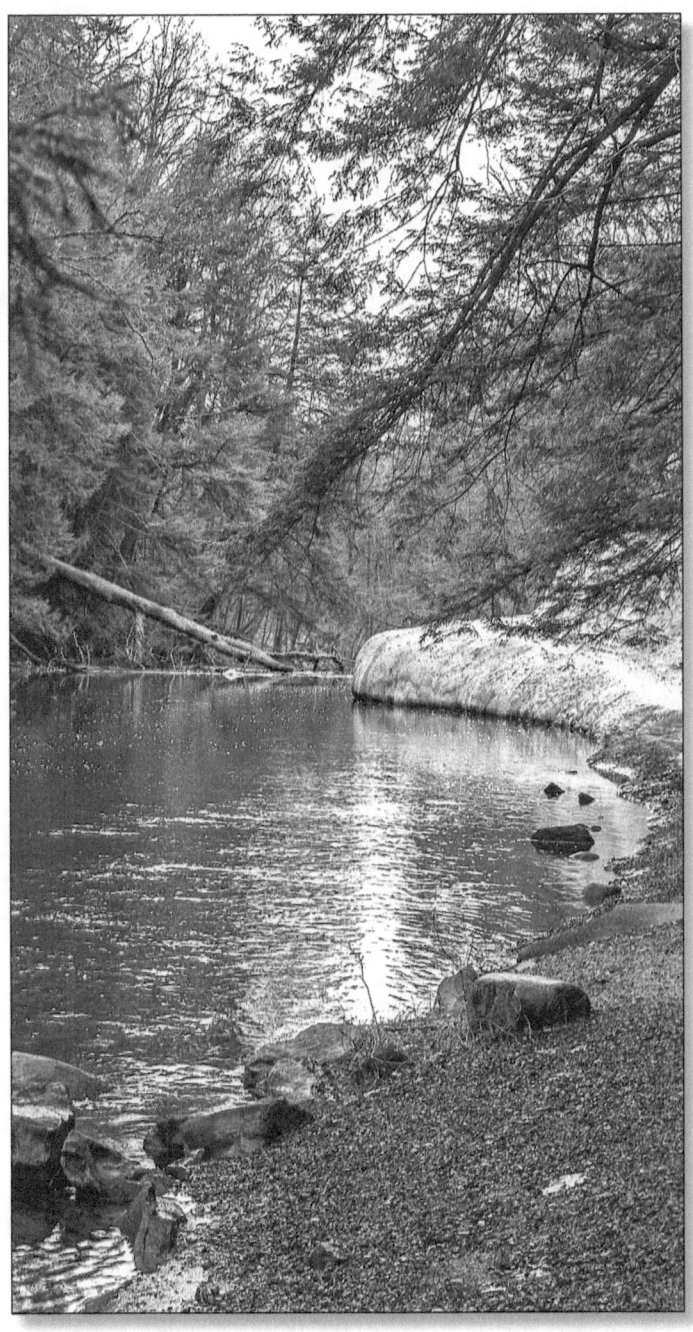

Saratoga Performing Arts Center, Saratoga Springs, NY, May 3, 2014
Canon EOS 20D, 46mm, 1/160, f/8, ISO 400, P, pattern metering
Photo © 2014 by Shawn M. Tomlinson

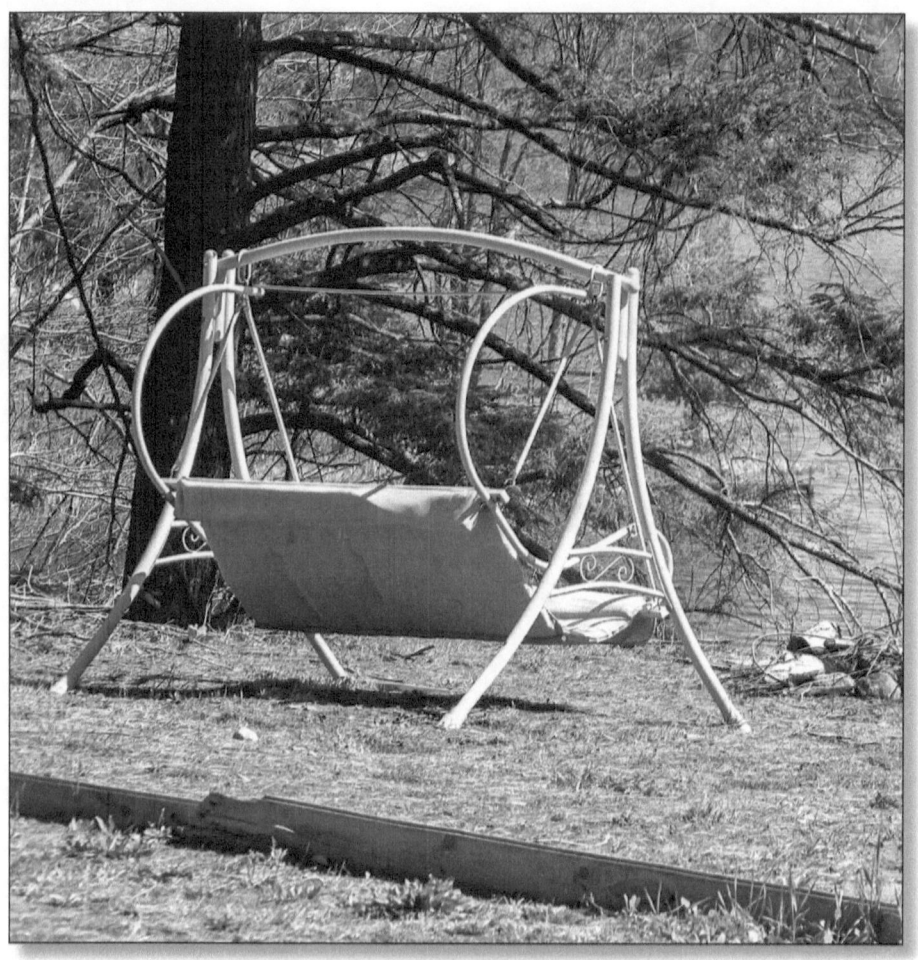

Galway Lake, Galway, NY, May 8, 2014
Canon EOS 20D, 116mm, 1/400, f/9, ISO 200, P, pattern metering
Photo © 2014 by Shawn M. Tomlinson

inks @ $62.95 each = $567 retail
 25 sheets 17-by-22 inches = $120
 So to start printing top-quality black and photos yourself, your initial outlay of cash would be approximately $1,982.
 3) Calibrate your computer display. Calibrating your display and coordinating it with your printer

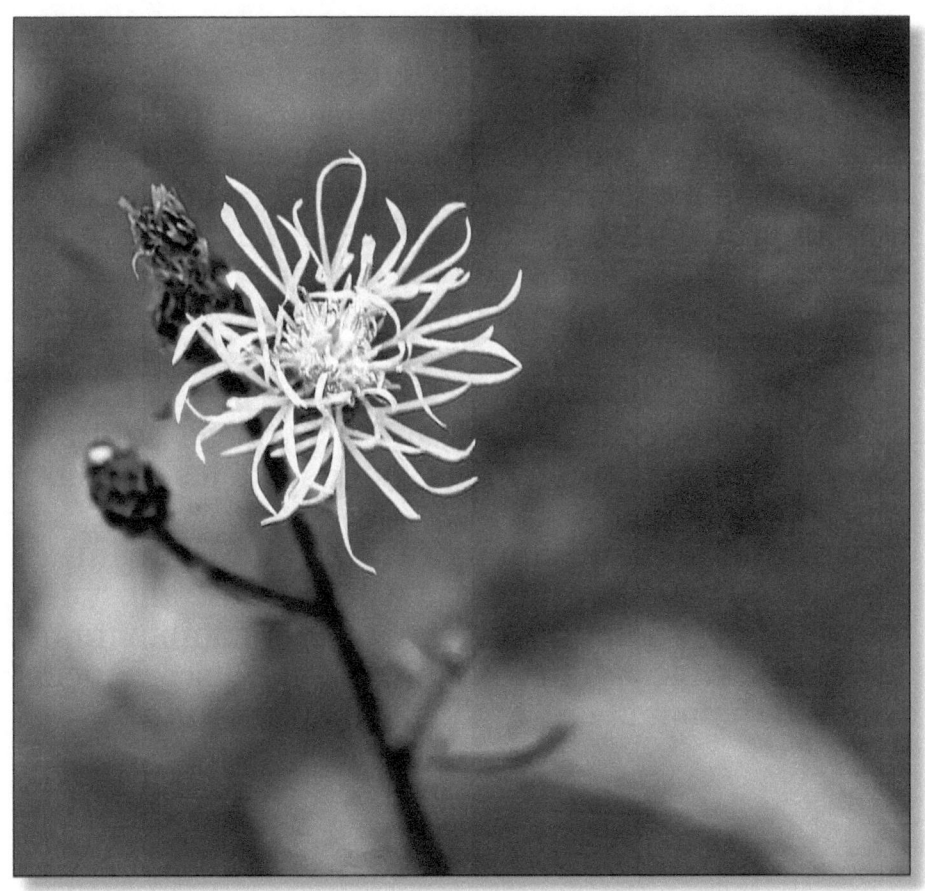

Fort Edward, NY, Aug. 9, 2014
Nikon D1, 250mm, 1/250, f/5.6, ISO 200, Av, pattern metering
Photo © 2014 by Shawn M. Tomlinson

— even a regular $100 printer — will go a long way
toward making what you see on your display match
what comes out of the printer. On a Mac, the System
preferences will give you a tool called Displays. This
allows you to set the calibration to the same color
space as Photoshop and your printer.

It still won't be perfect, but it will be closer.

One low-tech solution that you can try to make
better prints — color or black and white — and you

will have to experiment with it is to simply use the Levels panel in Photoshop to lighten the midtones. Doing this will make the image appear too light in many cases, but remember that because you are seeing them on a backlit display, they will be brighter than in print. Prints always will be darker than what you see on the screen.

There also are more elaborate systems for calibrating displays.

The key, really, is to match what you see on the display as closely as possible to what you get out the other end of the printer. This sounds like it should be easy, but isn't really.

However, as you print more black and white images, if you pay attention, you will learn the idiosyncrasies of the computer-display-printer combination. This will enable you to work around the discrepancies between them and create the prints you want.

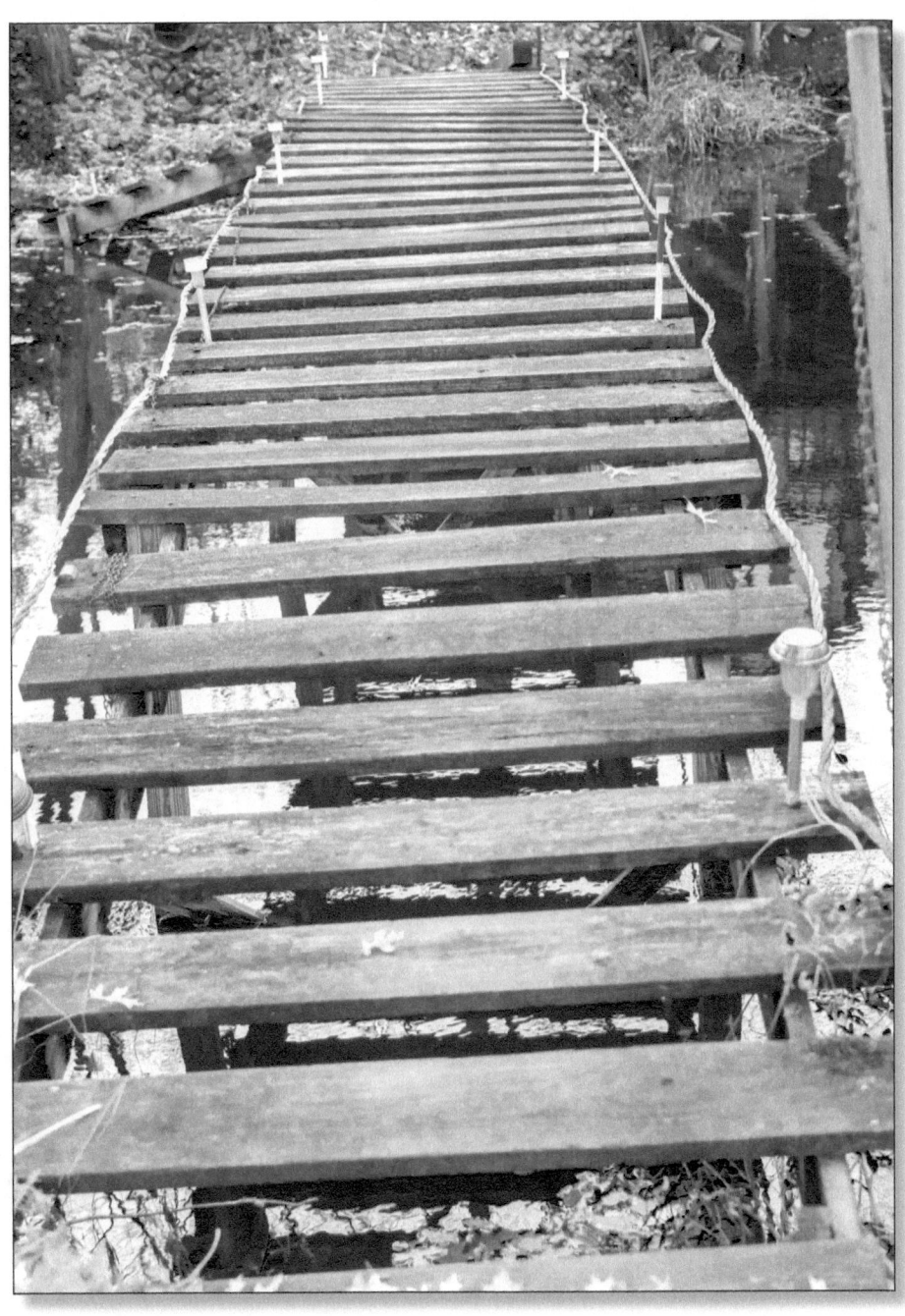

Schuylerville, NY, Nov. 8, 2014.
Nikon D7000, 35mm, 1/500, f/3.5, ISO 400, Tv, pattern metering
Photo © 2014, 2015 by Shawn M. Tomlinson

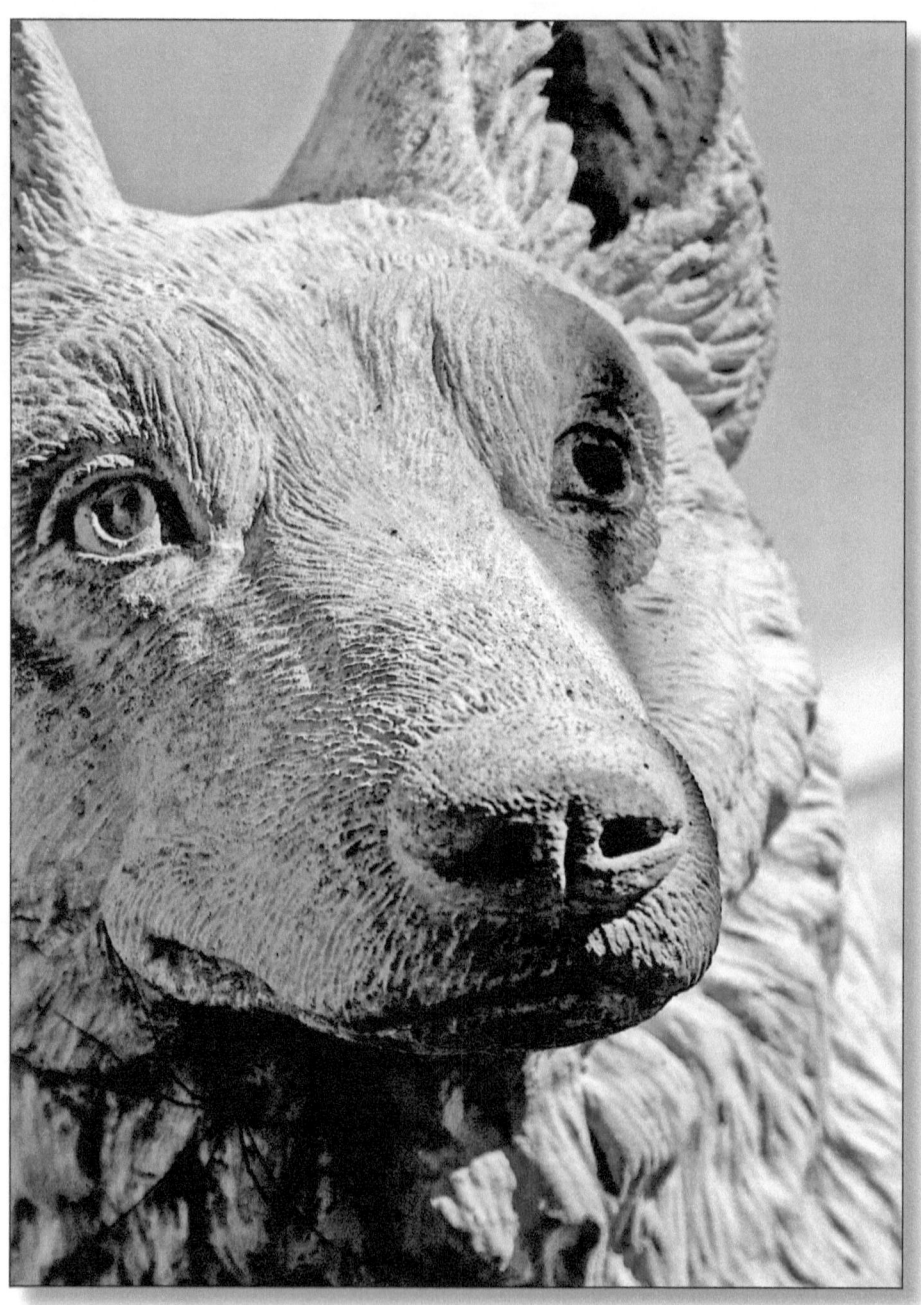

Greenwich, NY, Aug. 30, 2014
Nikon D70, 270mm, 1/1250, f/9, ISO 400, Tv, pattern metering
Photo © 2014 by Shawn M. Tomlinson

Part 8:
Ye Olde eBooke Shoppe

It is the second decade of the 21st century, so printing is not the be-all, end-all of photography as it once was.

It's still important, but you have a much greater opportunity to get your images seen by far more people than ever before by creating electronic display products. This could be anything from free website galleries to paid-for downloadable eBooks.

Just as an aside, you can publish your photo eBooks to Amazon for Kindle, but the Kindle in all its variations is not the best exhibition delivery device. Its shape does not conform to standard photo dimensions, the screen is relatively small and the Kindle formatting process makes it difficult to display images exactly as you want them to appear.

For example, the photos in the eBook version of *The Black & White Book* appear as they do because I take great pains to design and format them in such a way that the Kindle formatting process cannot — usually — undo what I've done.

I cannot place a photo with the cutline (caption) directly underneath it in the design and expect it to appear that way on the reading device.

So, to override this problem, I set up the photos in Photoshop, add a white or gray area beneath the image, place the cutline there and save the whole thing

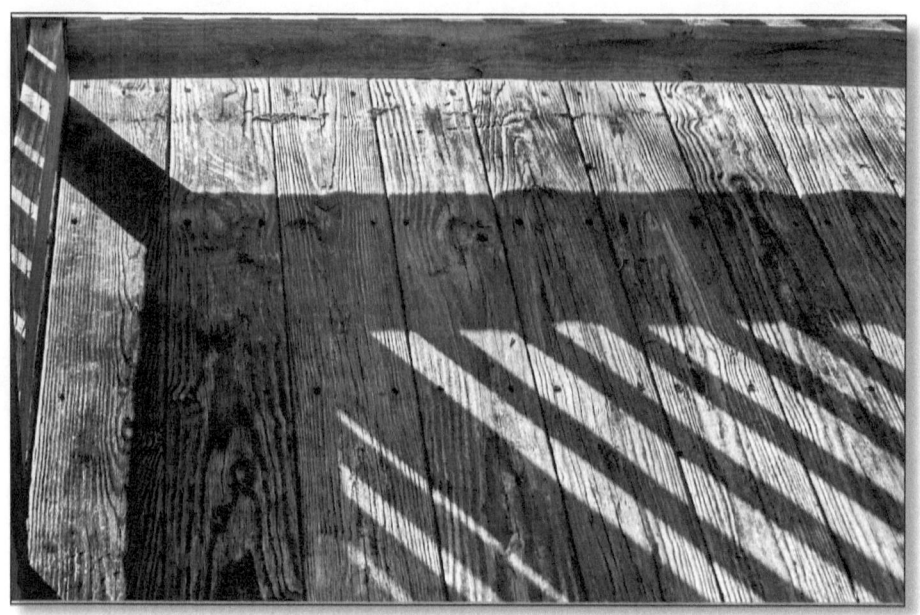

Ballston Lake, NY, May 1, 2014
Nikon D1, 60mm, 1/500, f/5.6, ISO 200, Av, pattern metering
Photo © 2014 by Shawn M. Tomlinson

as a JPEG image. This makes it virtually impossible for Amazon's formatting software to break the two apart.

One thing I have yet to figure out how to do is to place the images within the text where I want them to be. Doing this and then uploading the files for formatting for the Kindle shifts the text around and moves the photos to where I don't want them.

For this reason, I place photos at the beginning or end of sections. Coming from a print background, this annoys me because I cannot use the images to break-up large blocks of text, or to put the photos in the text where the text directly relates to them.

This is not Amazon's fault, nor the fault of the Kindle formatting software because the Kindle and other similar mobile devices are designed for more standard, heavy-on-the-text books rather than on those with many illustrations and photos.

It simply is the wrong type of device for displaying photos as the primary point of your eBook.

If I were a hardware engineer, I would design the mobile device equivalent of the former photo coffee table book, a device designed specifically to present photographs in the best possible way for eBook readers.

And, of course, if someone now actually does this, I will be thrilled and I will expect to see checks in the mail.

So, in the meantime, you still can create photo package eBooks designed specifically by you to give

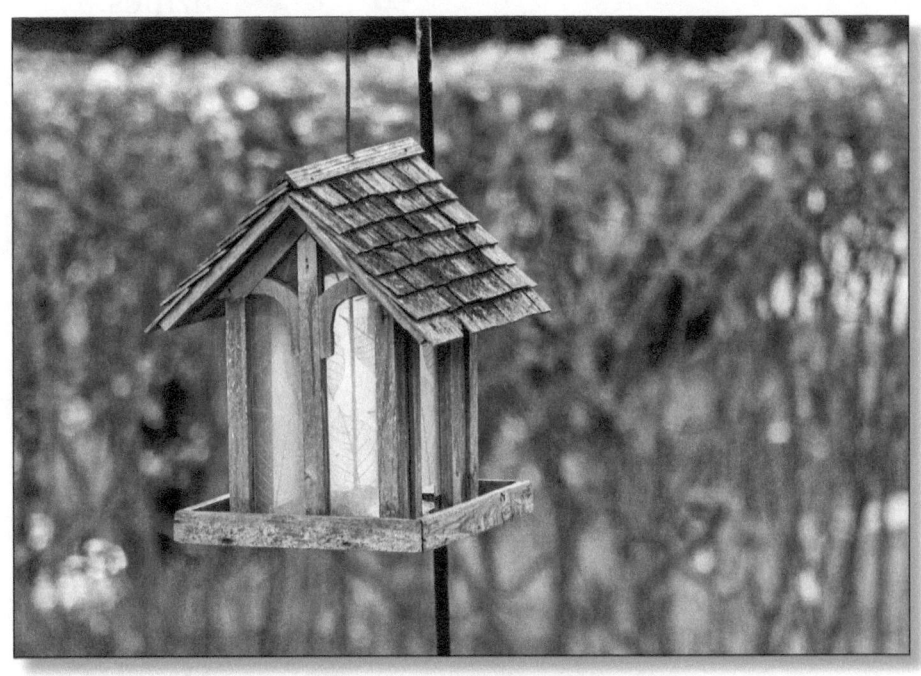

Ballston Lake, NY, Dec. 7, 2014
Nikon D7000, 240mm, 1/320, f/5, ISO 400, Tv, spot metering
Photo © 2014 by Shawn M. Tomlinson

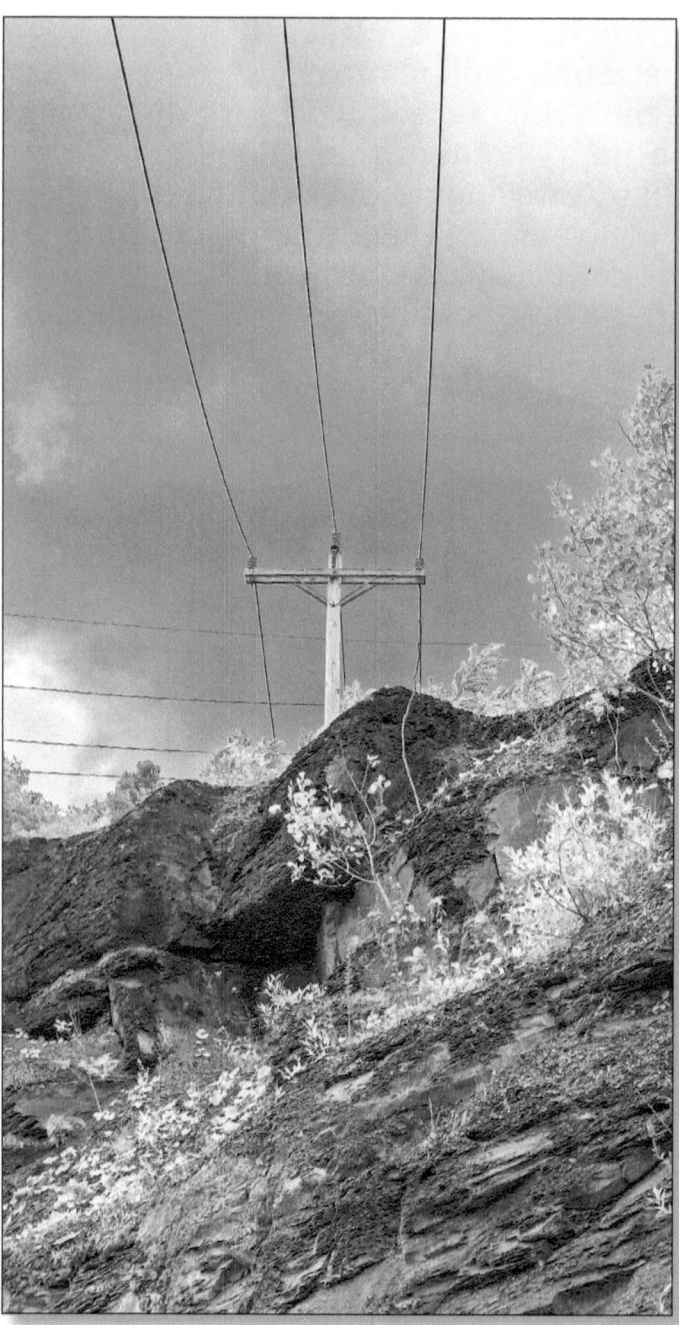

Fort Edward, NY, Aug. 9, 2014
Nikon D70, 52mm, 1/250, f/8, ISO 200, P, pattern metering
Photo © 2014 by Shawn M. Tomlinson

the world your black and white images in exactly the type of display you like.

As I may have mentioned, I have a long professional history in newspapers and magazines. I taught myself design and have worked for many years to improve my skills for my own publications as well as for those of others.

This mindset let me to create my first themed

photo eBook not that long ago.

My main design software at the time was QuarkXPress, but I could not figure out a practical way to design the types of eBooks I wanted in it.

Then my Mac Pro died and I did not have access to QXP for a while.

When the newer Mac Pro arrived, I had difficulties installing QXP on it at first, which led

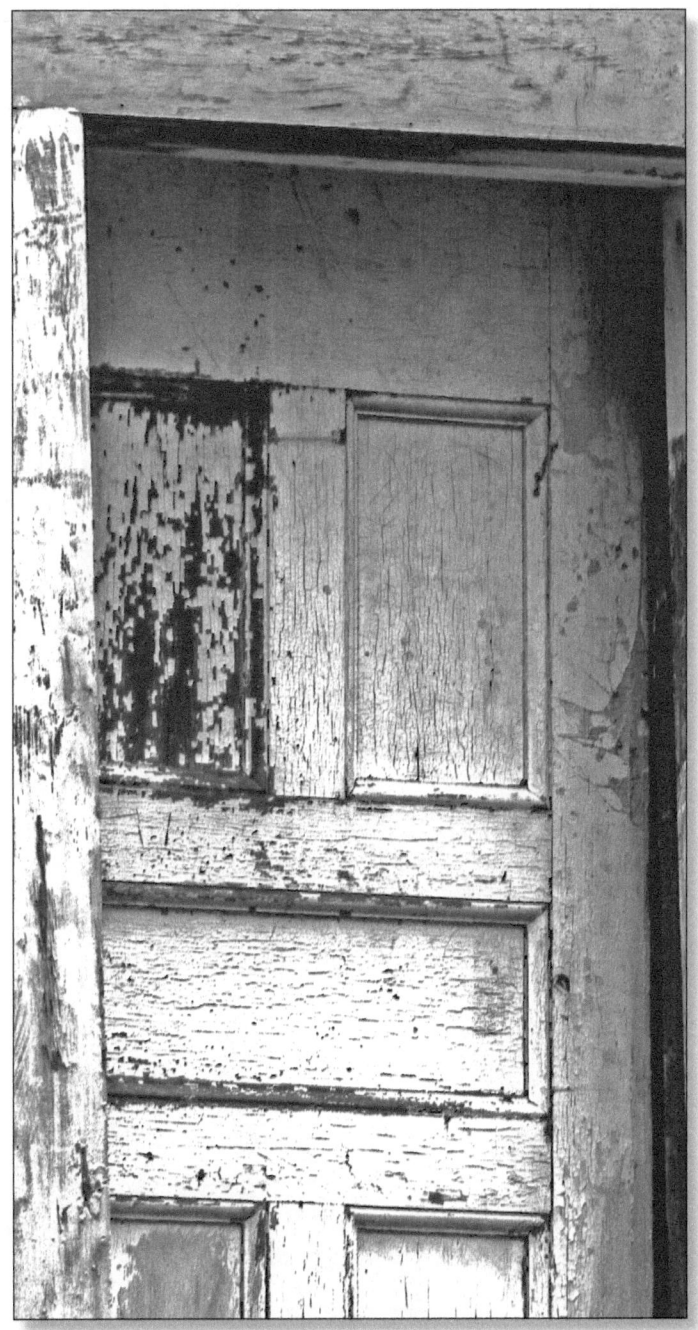

Saratoga Springs, NY, Aug. 23, 2014
Nikon D70, 300mm, 1/400, f/6.3, ISO 400, Tv, pattern metering
Photo © 2014 by Shawn M. Tomlinson

me to think that perhaps for this type of publication, I could do it in Photoshop itself.

Unlike all my other types of publications, photo eBooks have no need of running text from page to page. In fact, I reasoned, each photo should have its own page and this would, as Bela Lugosi once put it, "simplify everything."

Photoshop, though, is not really meant as a publication design program. It is intended to be used in conjunction with desktop publishing software, specifically Adobe's own InDesign, but also with QXP.

Virtually everything I knew from years of working with QXP wouldn't work in Photoshop, so I had to start from the ground up. After many aborted attempts, eventually I created the first one, titled *Pole Explorer*. Coming from a print background as I did,

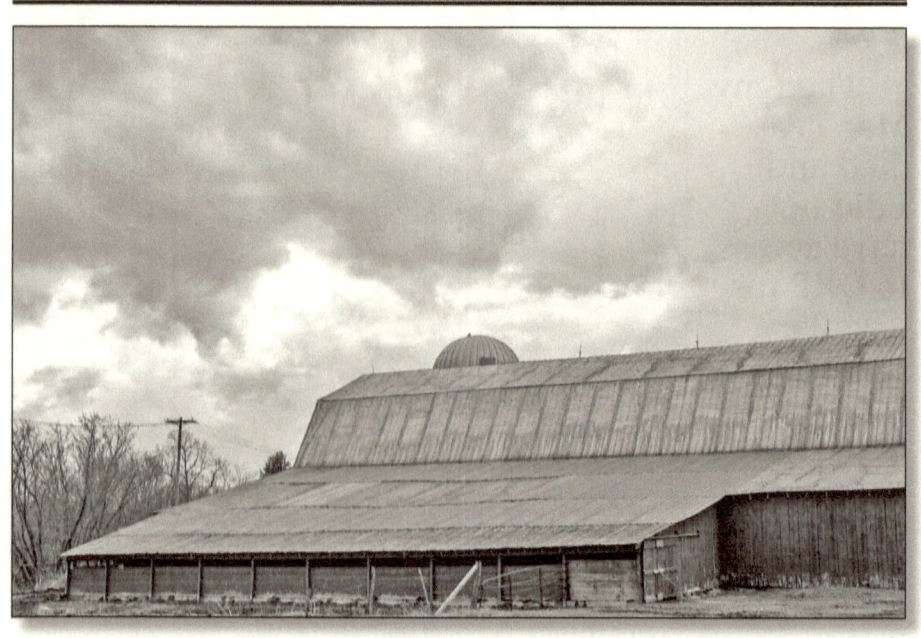

Burnt Hills, NY, May 1, 2014
Canon EOS 20D, 32mm, 1/250, f/10, ISO 200, P, pattern metering
Photo © 2014 by Shawn M. Tomlinson

I had in mind the rules about photos for printing. I made that first eBook 300 pixels per inch and that meant it had to be 15-by-15 inches in size. This created enormous files.

And it all was unnecessary.

An eBook is not going to be printed as-is. That's why it's an eBook.

And since most computer and mobile device displays do not show any higher resolution than 72ppi to 100ppi, the enormous size of the images and eBooks was unnecessary.

Eventually, even though it went against everything I knew about resolution and publishing, I convinced myself that I should do everything in 100ppi.

Other than saving hard drive space, working at this resolution means smaller files, which means they can

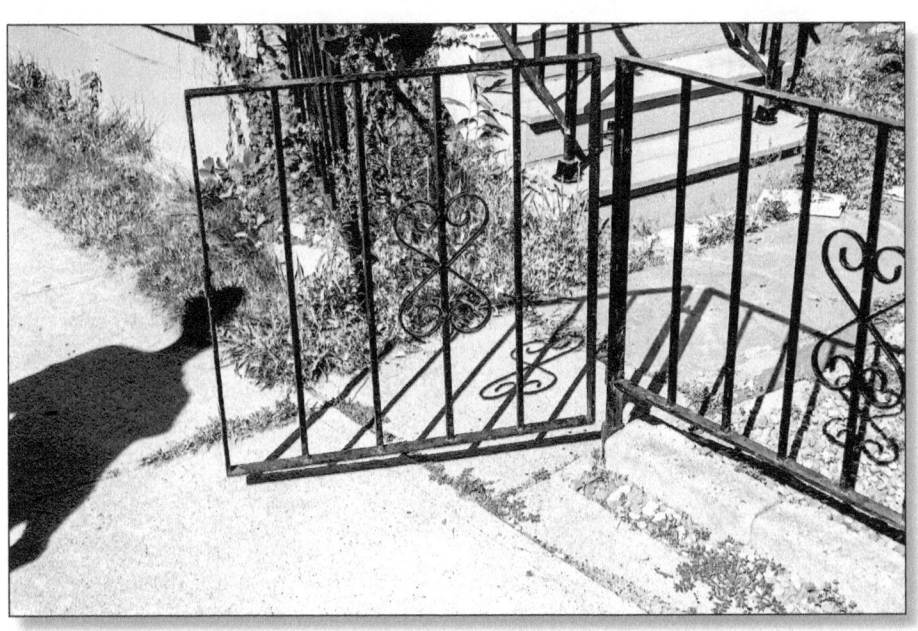

Gary Ziroli, Saratoga Springs, NY, Aug. 19, 2014
Canon EOS 20D, 35mm, 1/2500, f/4.5, ISO 400, Tv, pattern metering
Photo © 2014 by Shawn M. Tomlinson

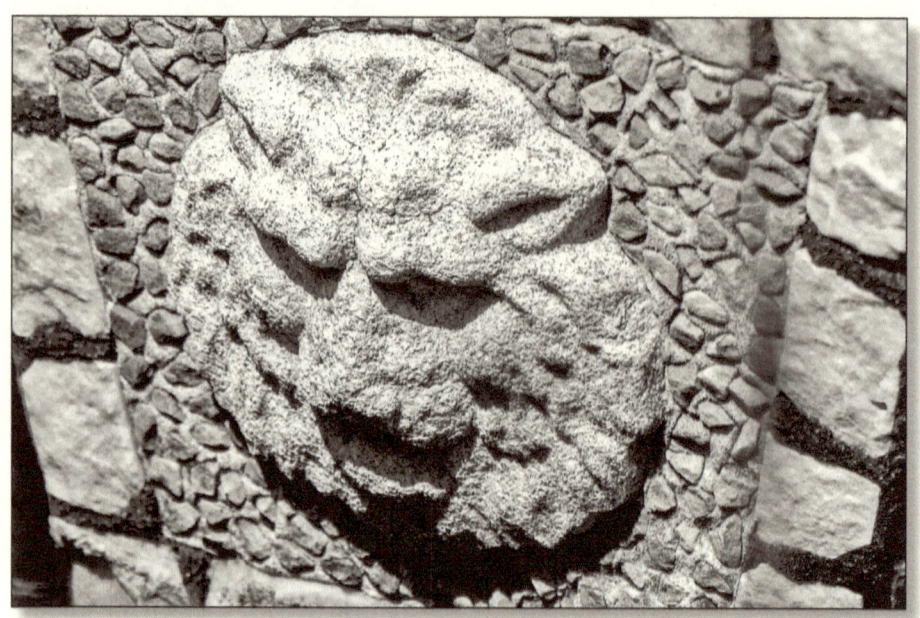

be emailed or downloaded.

Here's how I do it, and if you work with Photoshop and have a lot of patience, you can use this method, too.

1) I set up two templates, one for vertical and one for horizontal images. Both are the same square or near-square size, but they have different guides set up for there the images will be. They also have the cut-lines in different places so that I can get the biggest photo size that will fit on the page. So, for a vertical template, the cutline is over to the right of the image near the bottom. For horizontals, it can be in the same place or it can be moved to the center beneath where the photo will be.

Cutlines read like this:

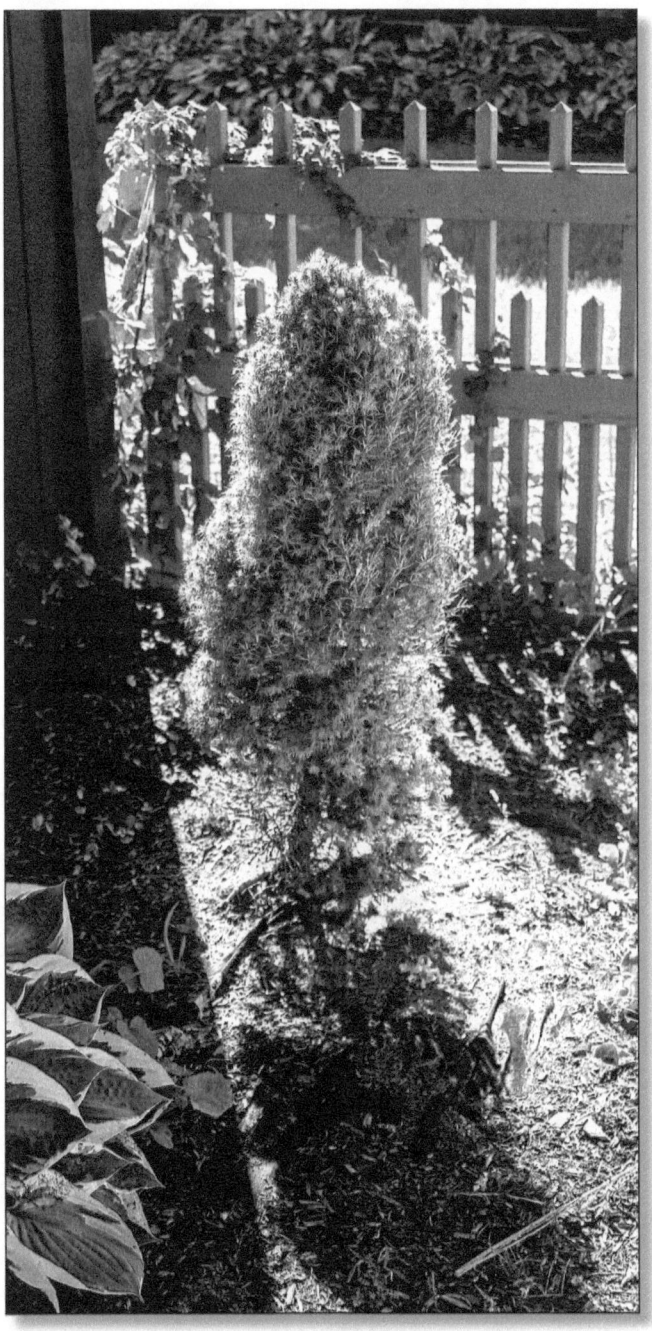

Joe Smith, Saratoga Springs, NY, Aug. 1, 2014

Because of the way these eBooks are designed, it is important to have your copyright information and name on each page. People still can steal your image, but this makes it a little bit harder without the craziness of watermarking your images and pages.

Saratoga Springs, NY, Aug. 19, 2014
Canon EOS 20D, 35mm, 1/2500, f/3.5, ISO 400, Tv, pattern metering
Photo © 2014 by Shawn M. Tomlinson

2) I then set a small

block of text to the left of the images for camera data. The casual viewer may not care what exposure, camera and lens I used, but other photographers do, so I include it. It's also a way to remember at a glance which combinations I used to get particularly good images.

This camera data section includes:

Camera: Nikon D7000
Lens: Nikon AF D 28mm f/2.8
Focal Length: 28mm (42mm)
Shutter Speed: 1/1000
Aperture: f/5.6
ISO: 400
File Name: 2014 1209 A BL D7k 015 DSC_9999

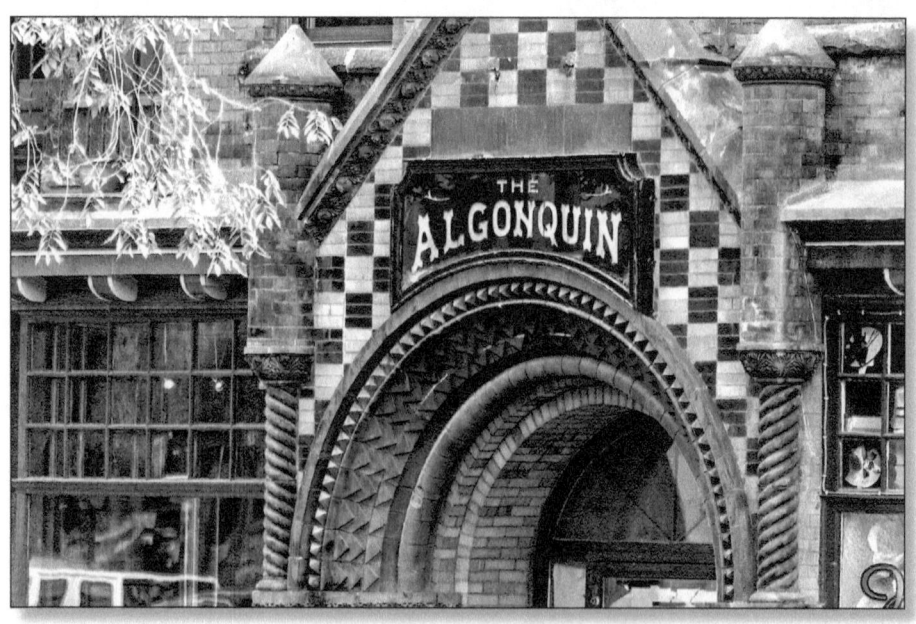

Saratoga Springs, NY, Aug. 23, 2014
Nikon D70, 250mm, 1/800, f/5.3, ISO 400, Tv, pattern metering
Photo © 2014 by Shawn M. Tomlinson

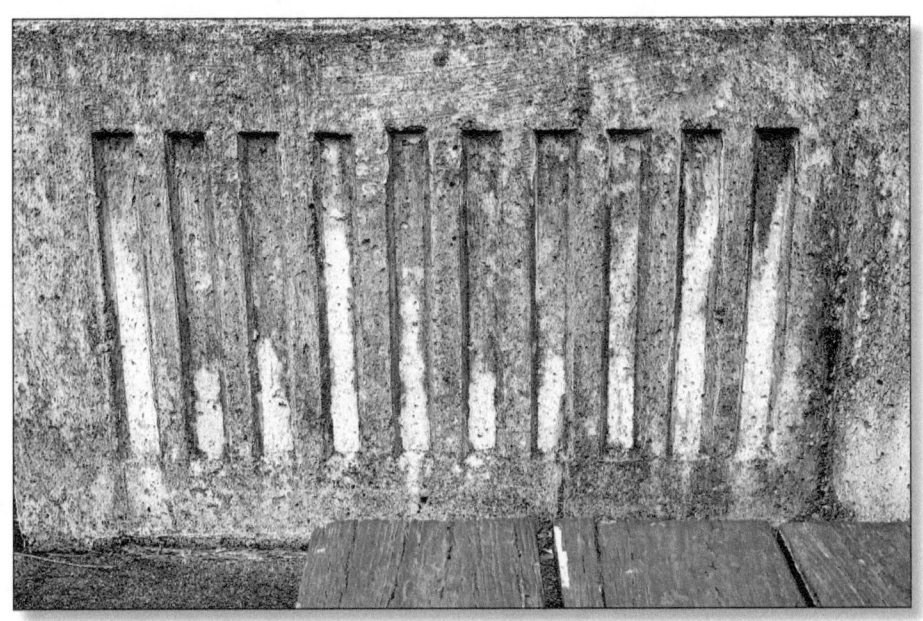

Saratoga Performing Arts Center, Saratoga Springs, NY, May 3, 2014
Canon EOS 20D, 28mm, 1/250, f/10, ISO 400, P, pattern metering
Photo © 2014 by Shawn M. Tomlinson

The number in parentheses for focal length is the actual focal length in full-frame or 35mm film terms. Obviously, if I'm shooting with a full-frame DSLR, there only would be one number.

3) At the top left of the templates I put the title of the eBook.

4) At the top right of the templates I put my name as the creator.

5) Each of these template page elements is a different Layer in Photoshop.

6) I select the images I want for the eBook. Because all of my images are saved a 300ppi TIFFs, to

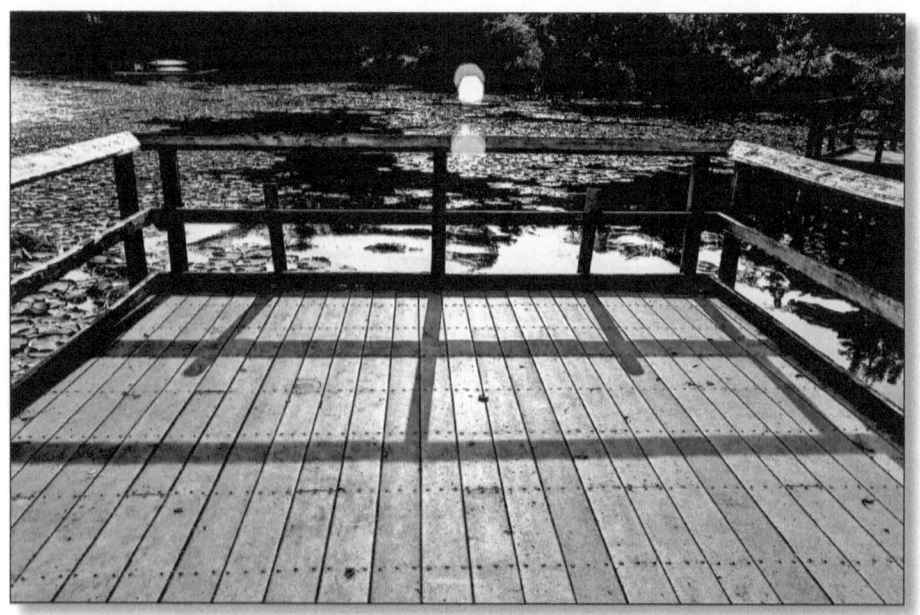

Ballston Lake, NY, Sept. 2, 2014
Canon EOS 1Ds, 28mm, 1/1000, f/10, ISO 200, Tv, pattern metering
Photo © 2014 by Shawn M. Tomlinson

get them to the correct size for the eBooks, they must be resized to 100ppi and saved as JPEGs to a different location. In other words, I'm making much smaller copies of the images and saving them to a specific, new folder where I can retrieve them easily and quickly to place them on the page.

In order to avoid making all these changes to each photo as I choose it, I set up an Action that resizes the image, saves it automatically to the new folder and closes it. This way, I just choose the image and click a button. Photoshop takes care of the rest.

7) Usually using one of the images I've selected for inclusion in the eBook, I design a cover for the publication based upon either the vertical or horizontal template.

8) I add a copyright page and sometimes an introduction page, again using one of the templates but deleting the Layers — cutline, camera data, etc. — I don't need.

9) I place the image, type or paste the cutline, add the camera data and save the template as a page number in the native Photoshop .psd file format. The reason for this is that it retains the Layers as separate elements. More than once I have made multiple pages only to realize I made a mistake on each one. When I was Flattening the Layers and saving the pages directly as JPEGs, it made it very difficult to fix these mistakes. If you still have all the Layers available, you can make corrections easily.

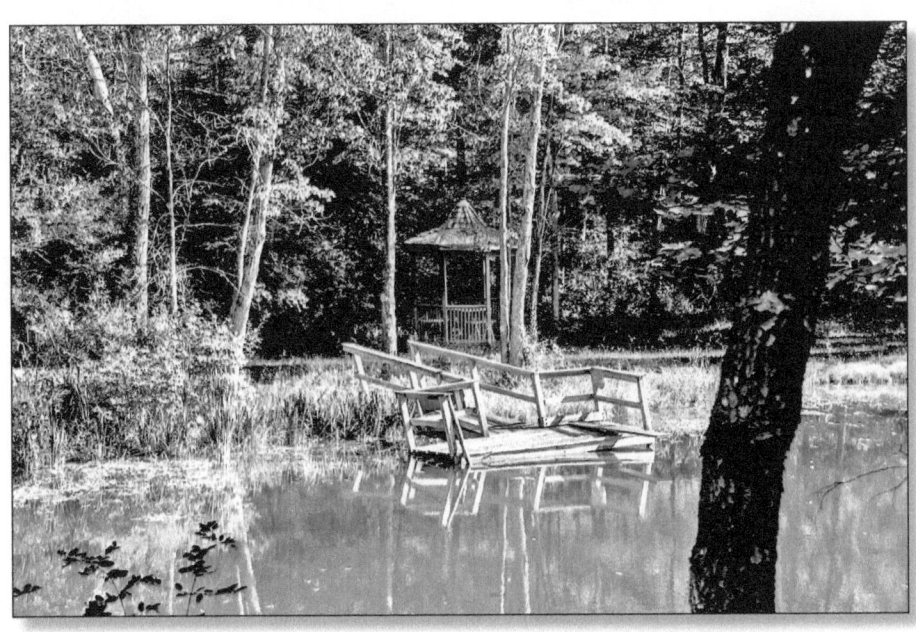

Galway, NY, Sept. 5, 2014
Canon EOS 1Ds, 80mm, 1/125, f/7.1, ISO 125, P, pattern metering
Photo © 2014 by Shawn M. Tomlinson

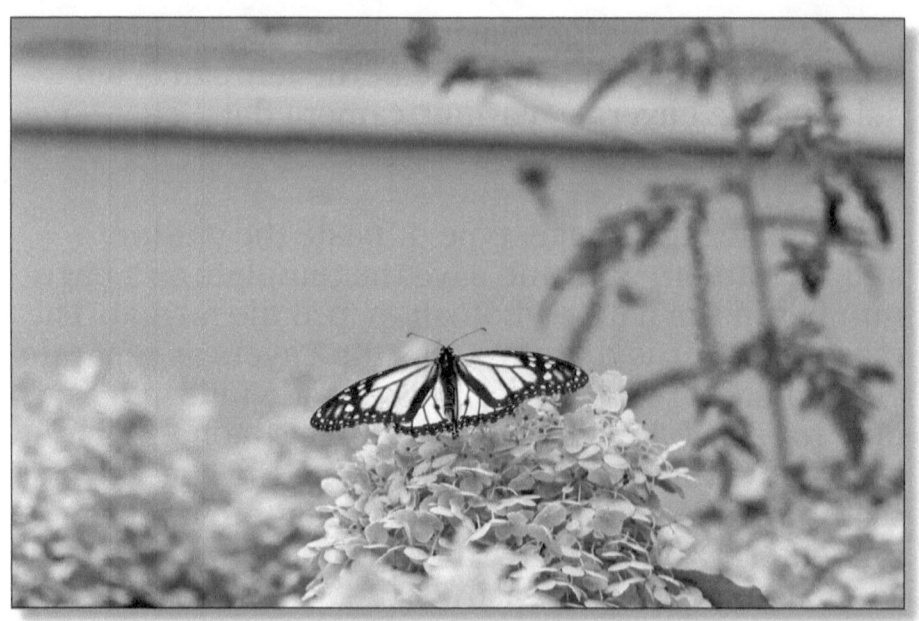

Saratoga Springs, NY, Aug. 23, 2014
Nikon D70, 300mm, 1/400, f/6, ISO 400, Tv, pattern metering
Photo © 2014 by Shawn M. Tomlinson

10) I make certain I save every page in the same manner as every other page in sequence. This is very important when you get to the PDF stage of this process.

So, the front cover page would be:

001 Explorer.psd

and every page thereafter, including the back cover will have the same name with the sequential page number, so:

001 Explorer.psd
002 Explorer.psd
003 Explorer.psd

The zeros in front of the number are important because they force Acrobat to put all the pages in the correct sequence. If you just use 1, 2, 3... 10, 11, 12... 101, 102 it throws off the page sequencing completely. Even if I'm certain I will not go to more than 99 pages, I still use the three-number sequence because it leaves me the possibility of adding pages without screwing up Acrobat.

11) When I finish with all the pages, I go to Bridge, open the Finished Pages folder I have been storing the page files in, select them all and then go to the Tools>Photoshop>Batch... menu sequence. This

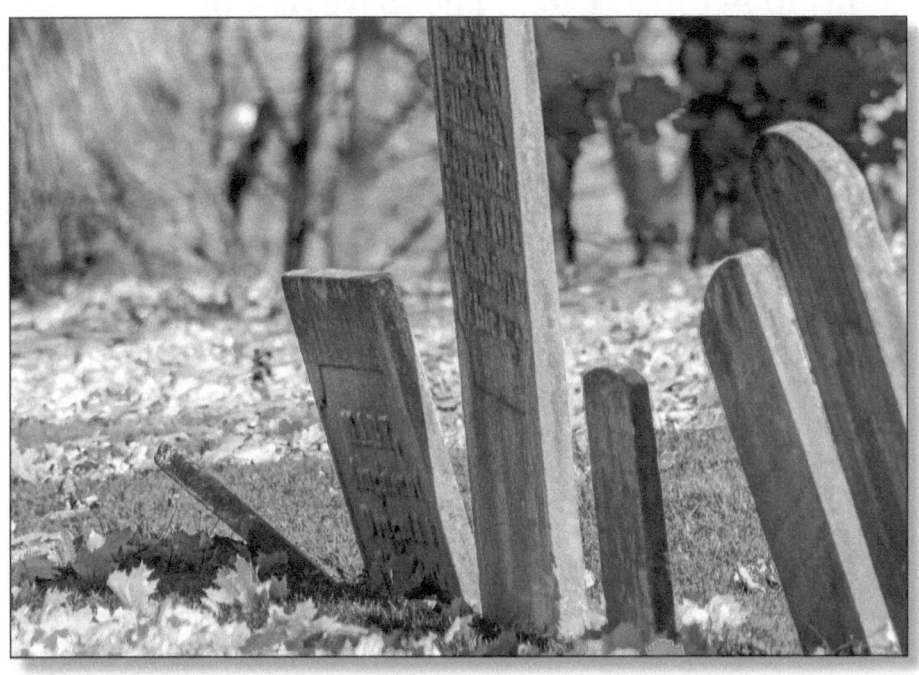

Johnstown, NY, Nov. 11, 2014.
Nikon D7000, 300mm, 1/1000, f/8, ISO 400, Tv, pattern metering
Photo © 2014, 2015 by Shawn M. Tomlinson

opens each page file in Photoshop, Flattens it and saves it as a JPEG to a folder within the Finished Pages folder.

12) I open Adobe Acrobat and go to Combine Files. I select all the JPEG page files and have Acrobat combine them into a PDF.

13) I save the created combined PDF, but I'm not quite done. Often, if your eBook is more than, say 25 to 30 pages, even keeping everything to 100ppi may not have saved you enough in file size. An eBook of 200 pages still will be too large to email and make downloading annoying. I need this version, but I will need something smaller for distribution.

14) In Acrobat, I go to File>Save As Other>Reduced Size PDF... In most cases using this option will compress the file enough to get it below 10mb.

As complex as all that may appear, once you've made an eBook or two, you will see it is time-consuming but not really that difficult.

It works, of course, for all photo, color, B&W, duo-toned, etc.

Last Words

Some of what is included here may seem to have drifted from the theme of black and white photography, but all of it is relevant and important as you consider becoming serious.

As I said, B&W photography is more than just clicking the Grayscale Mode button in Photoshop.

As you practice and experiment, you will find what works best for you, what types of images make the best black and

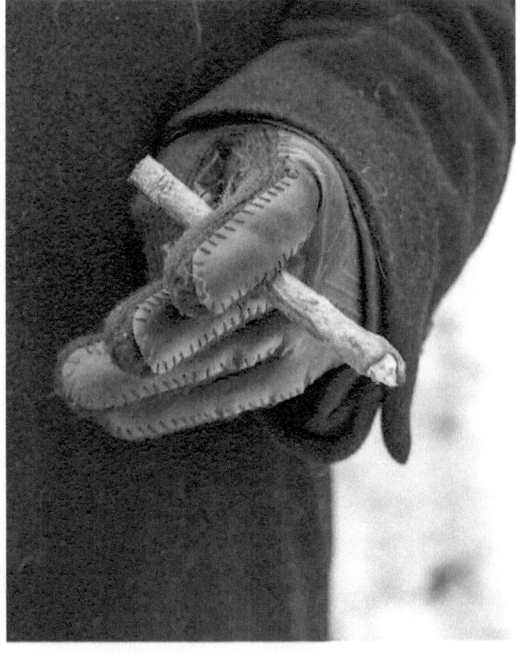

Shawn Tomlinson, Saratoga Springs, NY, Dec. 14, 2014.
Nikon D1x, 50mm, 1/80, f/4.2, ISO 400, P, pattern metering
Photo © 2014, 2015 by Gary W. Ziroli

white photos and many other things that will make you an expert in creating stellar art.

On last thing, an afterthought, if you will, is what I used to do frequently as a variation upon black and white images. It doesn't work for every photo and it may appear harsh, but for some subjects it will provide drama that will draw in the viewer.

After tweaking the sliders in the Black & White pane, try going to Image>Adjustments>Equalize. Then, go to the Filter menu and select Filter Gallery and go to the Distort section. Select Diffuse Glow and adjust the sliders as you choose.

Again, you most likely won't want to use this often, but it can give you some interesting images.

As you work with black and white images, too, you may find many more things that intrigue you and make your images work better.

You may like the Infrared preset (Image>Adjustments>Black & White>Preset: Infrared) or one of the Photo Filter effects or something I haven't thought of yet.

Presenting your images in your way is part of what makes it your art and unique.

— Shawn M. Tomlinson
Dec. 10, 2014

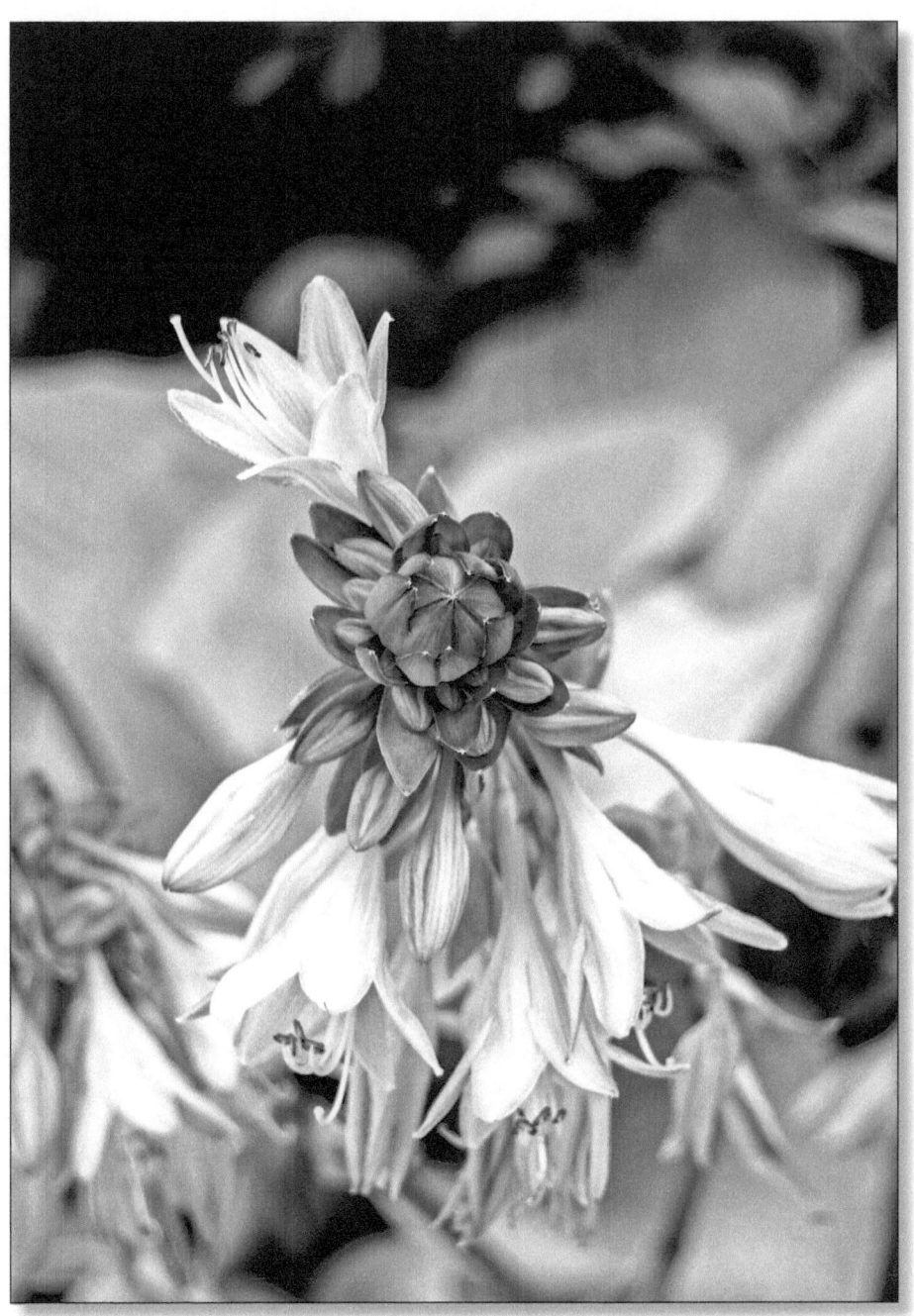

Saratoga Springs, NY, July 12, 2014.
Nikon D1, 80mm, 1/250, f/5.6, ISO 200, Av, pattern metering
Photo © 2014, 2015 by Shawn M. Tomlinson

The Black & White Book • Page 111

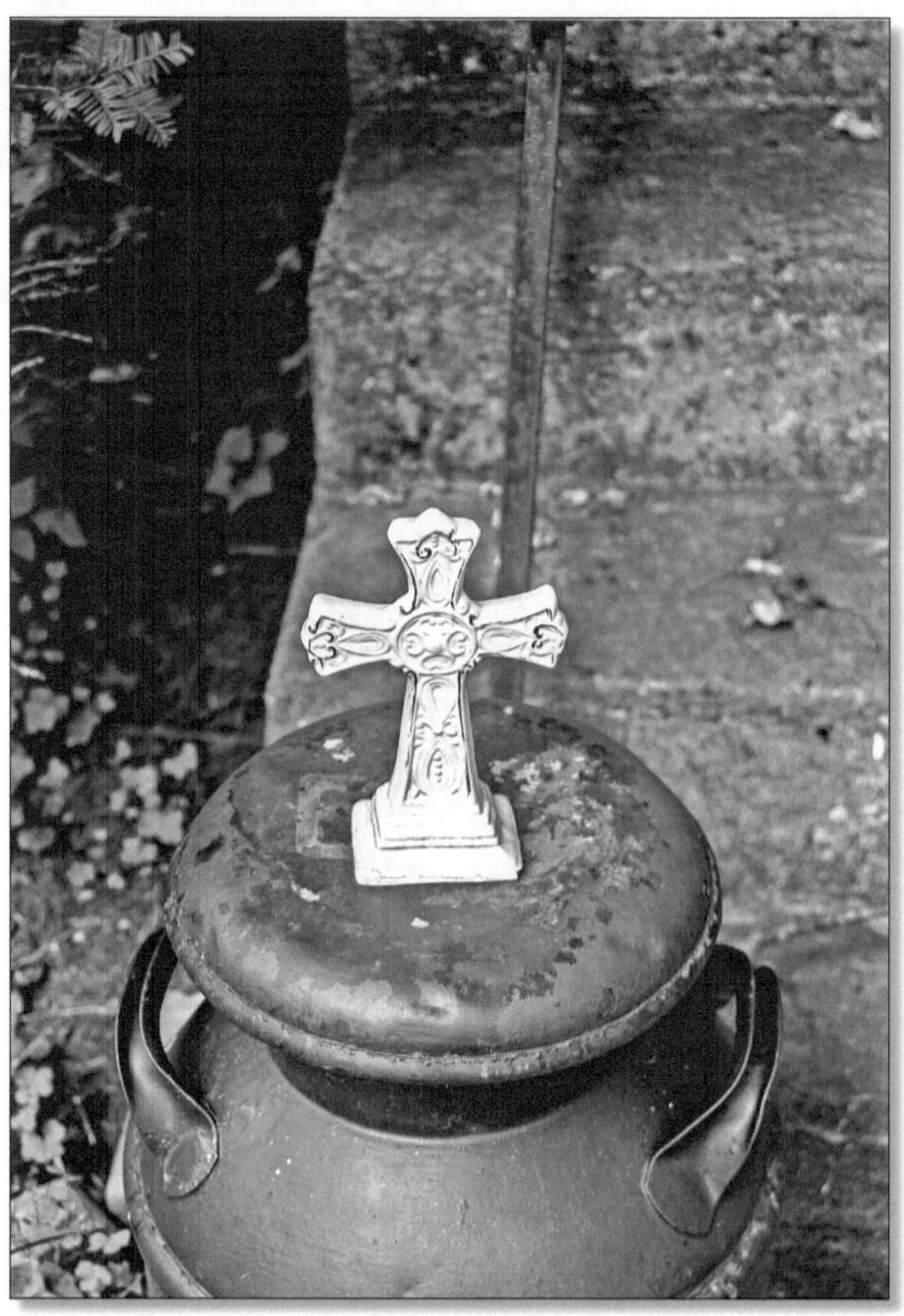

Ballston Lake, NY, Sept. 2, 2014
Canon EOS 1DS, 80mm, 1/125, f/7.1. ISO 200, P, pattern metering
Photo © 2014 by Shawn M. Tomlinson

Photographic Equipment

Since this is a book about photography for photographers, it stands to reason that the reader may want to know what kind of photographic equipment the author (me) uses.

And, hey, we photographers love talking about photographic equipment at least as much as about photographs.

All of this equipment is good and I have shot thousands of images with it. The cameras along with the exposure information is listed with each photograph in this book.

It has been an odd year for equipment for me. I have bought and used more of it than in any previous year, and I have had more problems with equipment than in any previous year. Here's the story, relatively briefly.

I started shooting with a Polaroid Land 420 in the early 1970s pre-puberty, made the transition to SLRs at age 14 in 1976 with the Cosmorex SE and Cosmogon 58mm f/2 prime lens. I stuck with that until 1982 when I became a Pentax user with the Pentax MX and Pentax 50mm f/1.7 prime lens. I stuck with the company into the autofocus film age with the PZ-10 and two Sigma zooms.

My first experience with DSLRs came in 2002

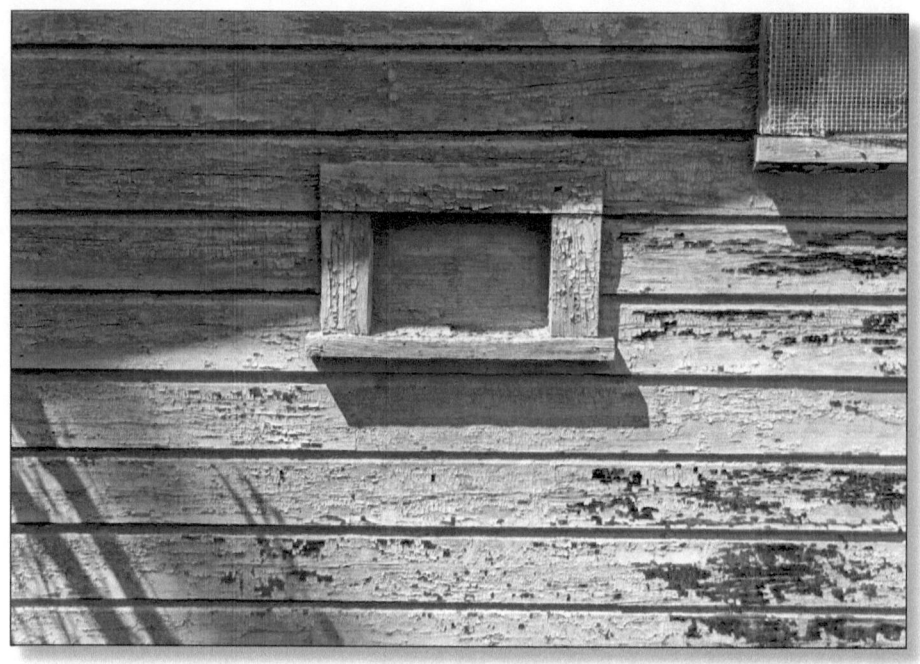

Saratoga Springs, NY, July 12, 2014.
Nikon D1, 28mm, 1/500, f/3.5, ISO 200, Av, pattern metering
Photo © 2014, 2015 by Shawn M. Tomlinson

when I needed to use the Nikon D1 owned by the newpaper for which I was the Sunday editor. The newspaper also had some dreadful Nikon Coolpix cameras I was forced to use when the D1 wasn't available.

By 2005 it was obvious I needed my own DSLR because I was shooting so much for the newspaper. I opted for the Pentax *ist DS which I still have. I sought a better DSLR in 2012 and purchased a Pentax K20D.

I was relatively content with Pentax when I discovered in 2014 that older DSLRs had gotten cheap. I decided that since Nikons and Canons finally were within my grasp, I would try them.

The Nikon D70 arrived and I got to it immediately.

The camera had problems, though, including difficulties reading and writing to memory cards sometimes, and a perpetually dirty sensor, no matter how many times I cleaned it. I worked around this for a while.

The Canon EOS 10D arrived next and I was blown away by the fantastic color.

I'd always wanted to own my own Nikon D1, but the price back in 2002 still was quite high, around $5,000. In 2014, I paid $57 for one.

Then, I paid way too much on eBay for a Nikon D1H that would not work.

Then, a month after I started using it, the Canon EOS 10D simply died during a photo shoot. I thought it was beyond warranty, so my wife, Carole, bought me a Canon EOS 20D to replace it. I decided to con-

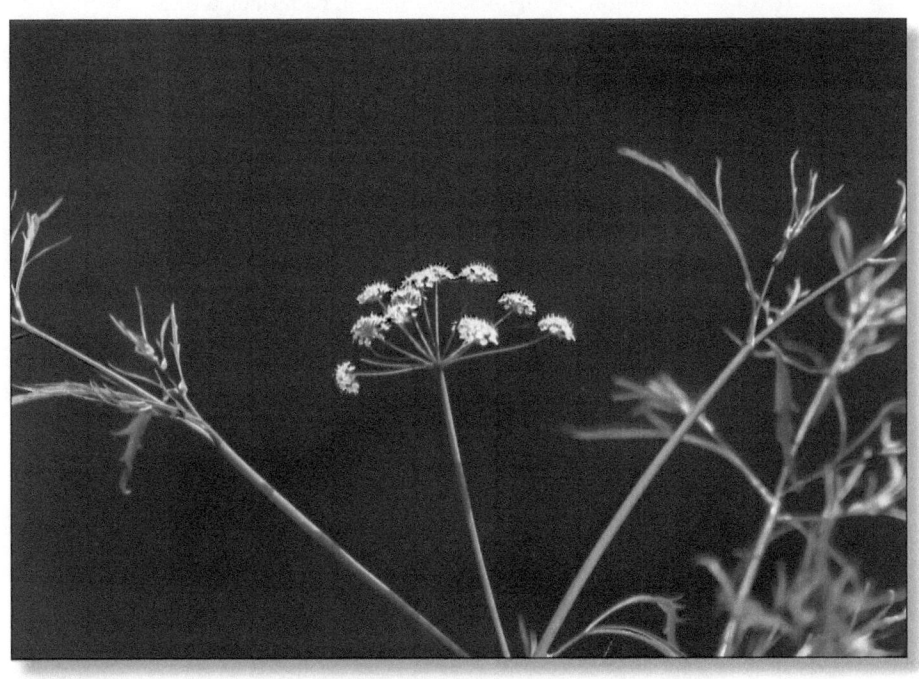

Mayfield, NY, Aug. 1, 2014.
Nikon D70, 300mm, 1/1600, f/6, ISO 200, Tv, pattern metering
Photo © 2014, 2015 by Shawn M. Tomlinson

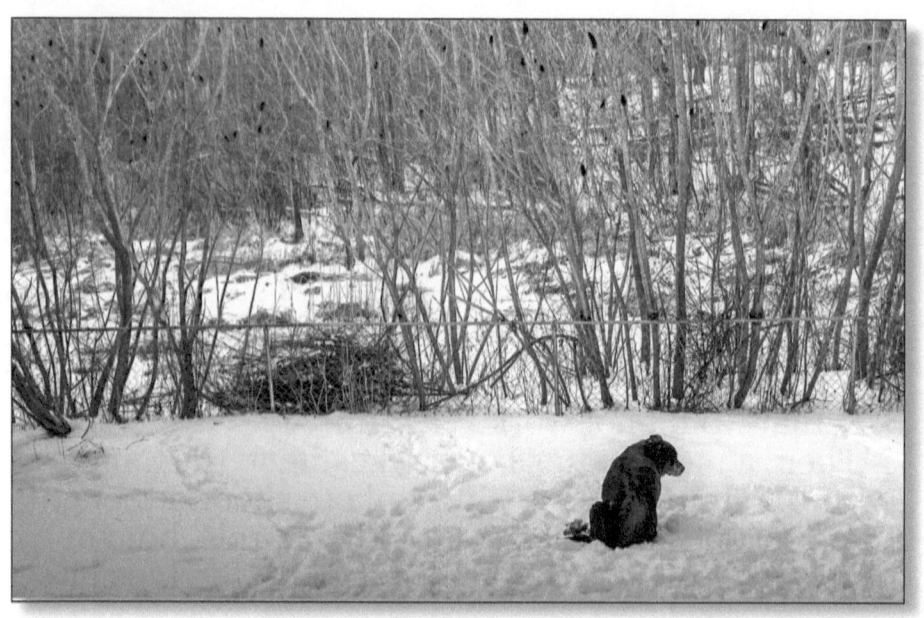

Baby, Ballston Lake, NY, Jan. 17, 2015.
Nikon D1x, 22mm, 1/160, f/3.5, ISO 200, M, pattern metering
Photo © 2015 by Shawn M. Tomlinson

tact the seller of the 10D — KEH, the same company I'd bought the D70 and 20D from — and they said no problem. They paid to have it shipped back to them and, since I'd already purchased the 20D, they refunded the money.

I had largely given up on the D70 because it recorded corrupted files sometimes, and had the dirt and memory card problems. Then, I thought, what the hell? I contacted KEH again and they paid to have it returned and sent me another one that works wonderfully.

Deciding to move to full frame, in late August, I purchased a Canon EOS 1Ds. From the start it had color banding issues, and once again, KEH proved itself a very honest company. I would have replaced the 1Ds with another one, but KEH didn't have another one at the time. So, my next choice was the Nikon D2X which suddenly had dropped in price.

Except, it was gone by the time I got the guy from KEH on the phone. The same day, for the first time, KEH had a Nikon D7000 that was much cheaper than they had been, just about the same price as I'd paid for the 1DS. I hadn't really thought the D7000 would be that great, but I accepted it.

I was wrong. It was that great. It was the best DSLR I ever used. I would have preferred it in a semi-pro body like the D300 because the semi-pros are tougher.

The reason I refer to the D7000 in the past-tense above is because it suddenly died after a couple of months. Again, KEH proved to be a fantastic company. They paid to ship it back to them and sent me one with a much lower shutter actuation count and it better condition.

I have used it extensively since it arrived — on a Sunday just before Christmas — along with the Nikon D2x pro DSLR I got a couple months later.

In addition to the DSLRs I've owned, I've also used a few owned by other people to test them. So here are the DSLRs in the order in which I used them:

Nikon D1, 2.65 megapixels, 2002-2009
Pentax *ist DS, 6.1 megapixels, 2006-present
Pentax K20D, 14.2 megapixels, 2012-present
Nikon D70, 6.1 megapixels, February-June 2014
Canon EOS 10D, 6.1 megapixels, March-April 2014
Nikon D1, 2.65 megapixels, April 2014-present
Nikon D1H, 2.65 megapixels, never, DOA
Canon EOS 20D, 8.2 megapixels, April 2014-present
Nikon D1X, 5.47 megapixels, June, July 2014
Nikon D70, 6.1 megapixels, July 2014-present

Nikon D300, 12.2 megapixels, August 2014
Canon EOS 1DS, 11.1 megapixels, Sept. 2-9, 2014
Nikon D7000, 16.2 megapixels, Sept. 22-Dec. 9,
2014
Nikon D7000, 16.2 megapixels, Dec. 22,
2014-present
Sony A100, 10.2 megapixels, Jan. 8, 2015-present
Nikon D2x, 12 megapixels, February 2015-present

As for lenses:
For the Pentax *ist DS and K20D
SMC Pentax DA 18-55mm f/3.5=5.6
SMC Pentax FA 80-200mm f/4.7-5.6
Sigma D 18-200mm f/3.5-6.3
SMC Pentax M 50mm f/1.7

For the Nikon D70, D1, D7000
Nikon AF D 28-80mm f/3.5-5.6
Nikon G DX 18-55mm f/3.5-5.6
Nikon AF D 28mm f/2.8
Tamron D LD 70-300mm f/4-5.6
Nikon G 35mm f/1.8
Nikon AF D 50mm f/1.8

For the Canon EOS 10D, 20D, 1DS
Canon EF II 28-80mm f/3.5-5.6
Canon EF III 28-90mm f/3.5-5.6
Tamron 28-200mm f/3.5-6.3
Canon EF II 50mm f/1.8

For the Sony A100
Quantaray 75-300mm f/4.5-5.6
Minolta Maxxum 50mm f/1.7

As far as software:
Adobe Bridge

Adobe Photoshop CC 2014
Adobe Acrobat
Adobe InDesign
Adobe Muse
Apple iPhoto
Adobe Lightroom (grudgingly)
Gimp
Seashore

I run everything on an Apple Mac Pro, Early 2008, 8-Core, 2.8GHz, with 32gb of RAM.

That list should satisfy even the most obsessive-compulsive photographer-techno-geek, like me.

If you're wondering why I use the old, much lower resolution DSLRs, well, look at the photographs in this book. I notice a slight sharpness increase as the megapixels multiply, but I get fantastic shots even with the 2.65-megapixel Nikon D1.

See my book titled *Retro Camera Buying Guide: Getting Serious About Photography... On the Cheap!* for suggestions about how you can get great images with these old DSLRs. It covers the entry-level DSLRs.

— SMT, May 29, 2015

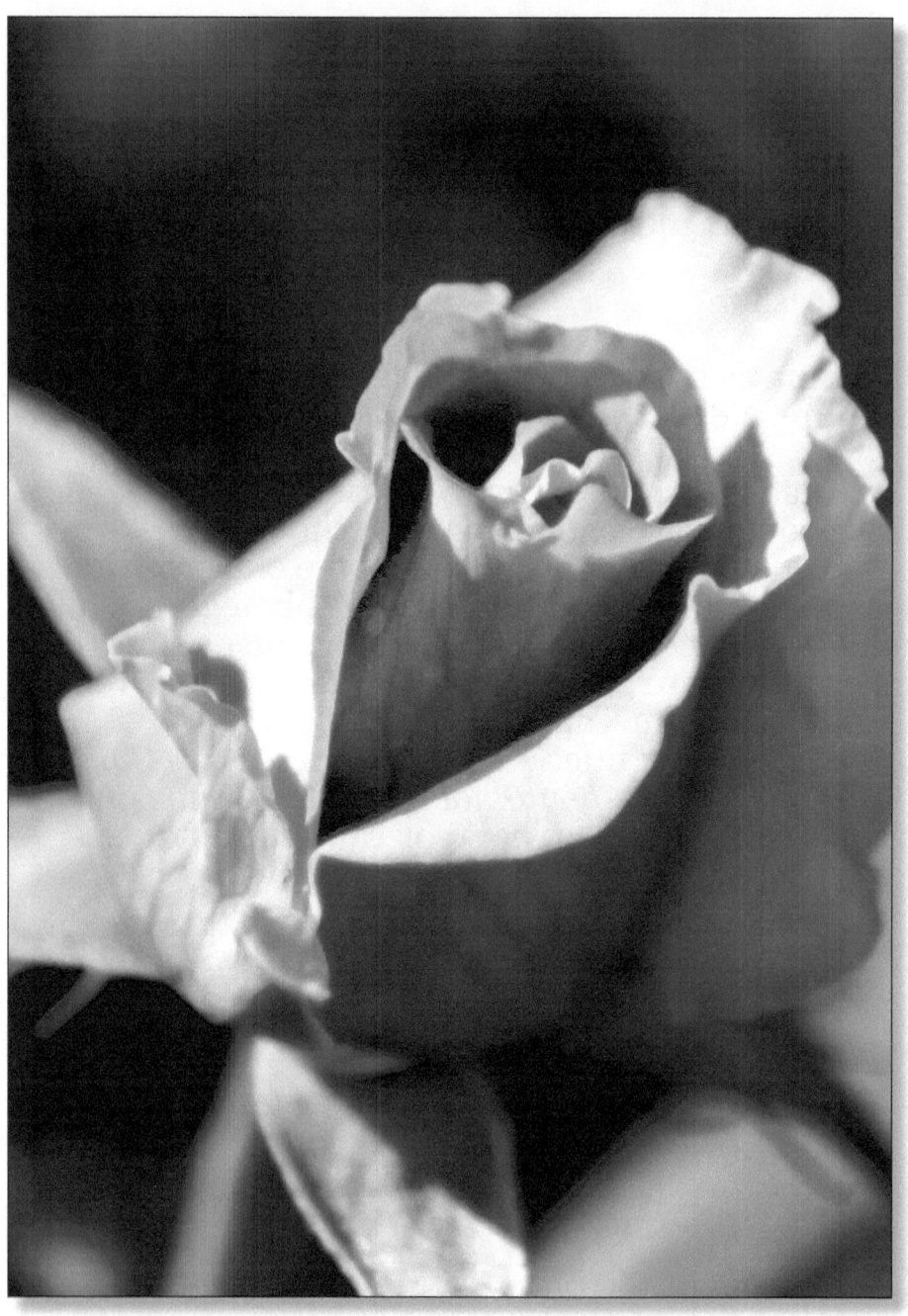

Rose Garden, Central Park, Schenectady, NY, Aug. 17, 2014.
Nikon D70, 300mm, 1/5000, f/6, ISO 250, Tv, pattern metering
Photo © 2014, 2015 by Shawn M. Tomlinson

Shawn M. Tomlinson's Guide to Photography Series

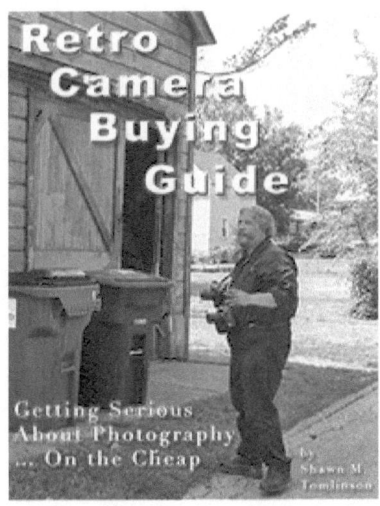

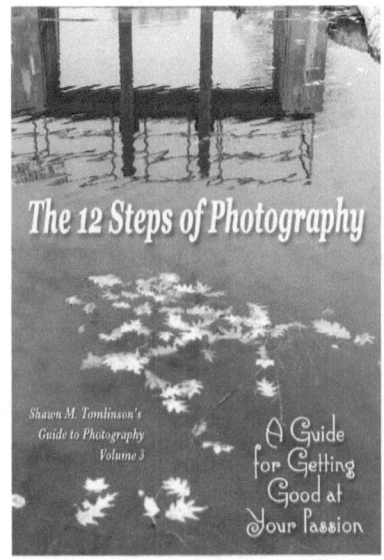

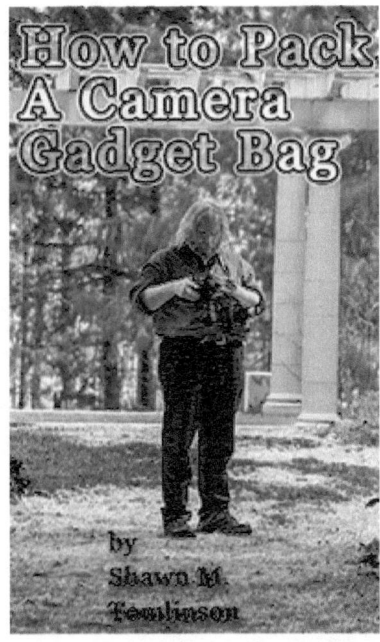

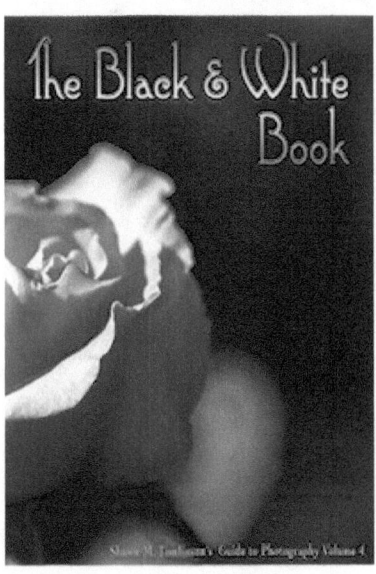

Shawn M. Tomlinson's Guide to Photography Series

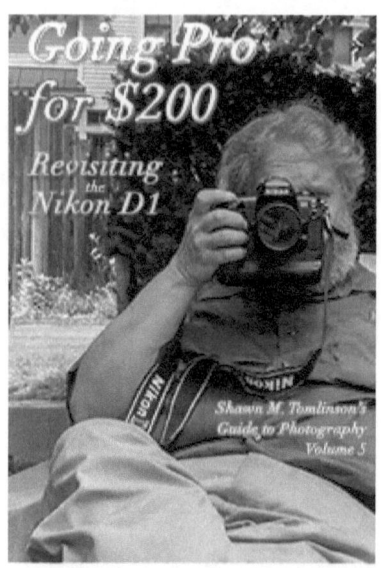

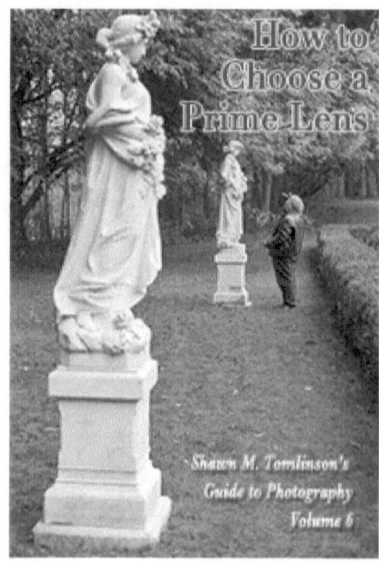

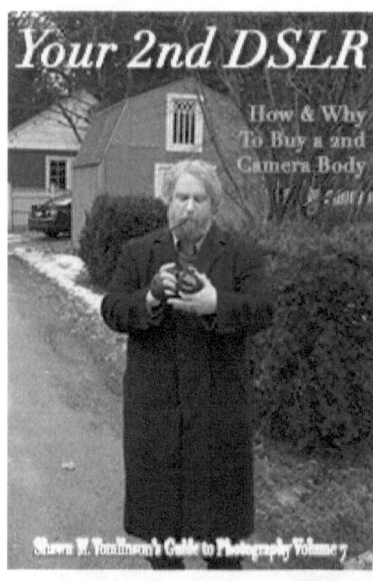

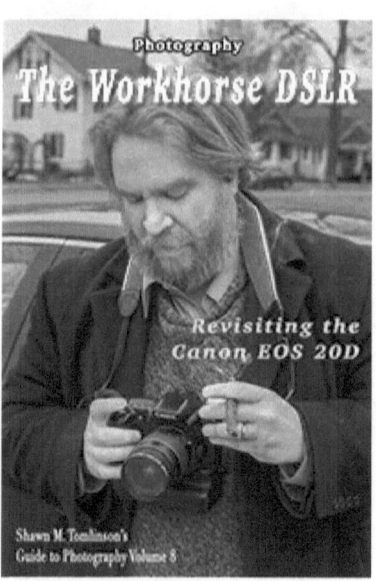

Shawn M. Tomlinson's Guide to Photography Series

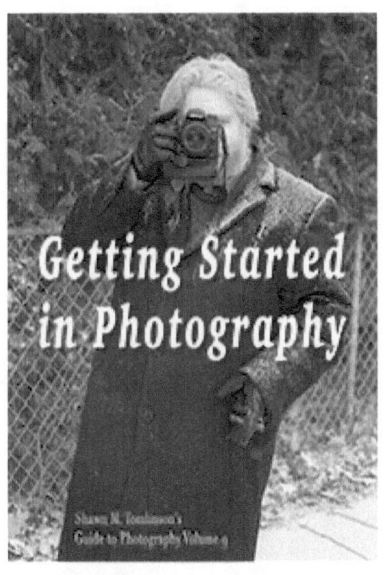

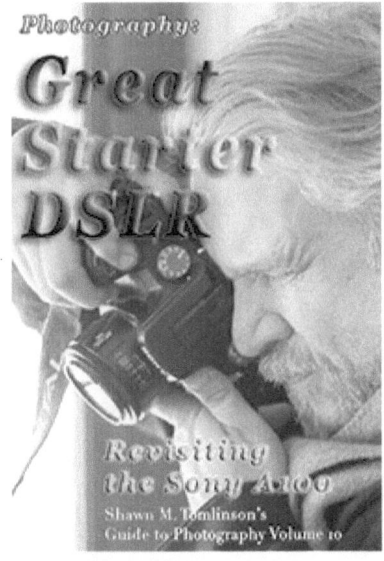

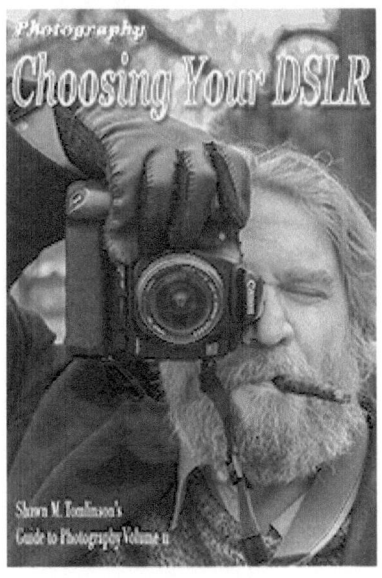

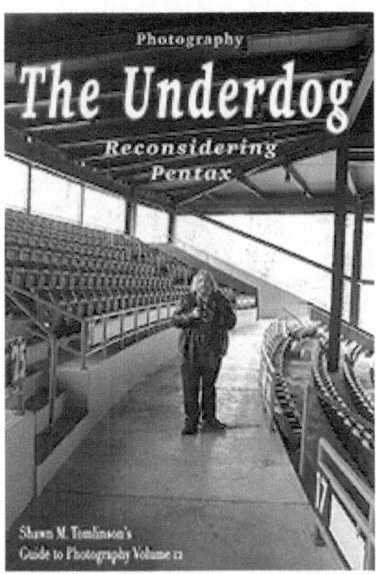